HOT ROD
MAGAZINE

JULY 1951 25c

V8s — From FORD to "FIREPOWER"

By Don Francisco

★ ★ ★

DRAG STRIP DIFFICULTIES

Sirs:

Around here there is an old abandoned air field. It has three or four long runways. Awhile back, to be exact about four months ago, all the rods gathered at this air strip, which is called Kurtis Field, to have drag races. Finally, week after week, talk spread around and huge crowds came to enter and to watch the meets. They were terrific!

We really had it organized nicely. The police even came down on Sunday afternoons to watch us. They too were enthused as long as we kept our heads about things. But of course in every crowd there has to be a wise, peculiar person. While we were having drags, this wise guy had to rev his motor and start showing off in the sidelines. He would wind up. then spin out a few times, etc. Finally he overdid it and spun out and flipped a couple of times, hurting himself and smashing into a beautiful rod. The car that flipped was a '49 Merc. Now he's spoiled it for everyone. The police came over and had to clear the entire field. Well. that ruined it. Now there are no more meets and everybody is going crazy.

What shall we do? The police now think all the accidents which occur are us rods. I love rods—I'm not against them. If only we could do something around here to let people recognize us instead of always faulting us.

Andrew S. Southard Jr.
Oceanside, L.I., New York

It might be wise to try following the pattern described in the article which appears on page 24 of this issue.—ED.

HOT RODS
of the
1950s

Andy Southard, Jr.

Motorbooks International
Publishers & Wholesalers ®

First published in 1995 by Motorbooks International Publishers
& Wholesalers, PO Box 2, 729 Prospect Avenue, Osceola, WI
54020 USA

The information in this book is true and complete to the best of our
knowledge. All recommendations are made without any guarantee
on the part of the author or Publisher, who also disclaim any
liability incurred in connection with the use of this data or specific
details

We recognize that some words, model names and designations, for
example, mentioned herein are the property of the trademark
holder. We use them for identification purposes only. This is not an
official publication

Motorbooks International books are also available at discounts in
bulk quantity for industrial or sales-promotional use. For details
write to Special Sales Manager at the Publisher's address

Library of Congress Cataloging-in-Publication Data

Southard, Andy,
        Hot rods of the 1950s / Andy Southard, Jr.
                    p.   cm.
        Includes index.
        ISBN 0-7603-0055-0
        1. Hot rods. I. Title.
    TL236.3.S68   1995
    629.288--dc20   95-388

On the front cover: One of my favorite pictures of my early days of
owning my first Roadster was taken by friend Bob Walls in August
1955. Would you believe I told him where to stand? I focused my
camera, then climbed back into the Roadster, and snap, this nice result!

I was parked out in the middle of the cul–de–sac street, because
Bob took me over to meet famous race car driver and buddy of his,
Bill Peters. Bill was a ten-year veteran of racing and a top spectator
drawing card from 1946–1951. Bill had raced against Bob
Sweikert, Ed Elisian, and Bob Veith. With the decline of hot rod
racing, he switched to sprint cars. Bill moved away from Salinas,
and I haven't seen him since.

On the back cover: Jim Russell of Salinas, California, owns this 1933
Ford three-window Coupe. He has had the Coupe since he was in
high school, when I first met him. I often saw him cruisin' Main Street
and going to Mel's Drive–In, our favorite hang-out at that time.

Through all the years that he has had the Coupe, it has been painted
purple, raspberry, and lime. I pinstriped his Coupe three times
through the years. This picture does not show pinstriping. The
Coupe is purple now with my pinstriping still on from years ago.

The Coupe has a hopped-up '48 Merc engine, '39 Ford
transmission, and a '33 Ford rear end with 3.78 gear ratio. A true
Hot Rodder at heart!

Upholstery is white vinyl done by Manger of Castroville, California,
who is still in business. During the summer months at Roy's Drive–In,
on Graffiti Night, you might see Jim in his outstanding Coupe.

On the frontispiece: In the first couple months of 1951, I wrote
a letter to the editor of *Hot Rod* telling of our drag strip
difficulties. Much to my surprise, my letter was printed in the
"In The Bag" column of the July 1951 issue. Take note of the
magazine price at that time.

Little did I realize that this letter would not be the last thing of
mine to be published in *Hot Rod, Car Craft, or Rod & Custom*, to
name a few. I never would have dreamed that twelve years later I
would be affiliated with *Rod & Custom* as managing editor, and
would be contributing pictures and storyline for nineteen years. It
was indeed a pleasure, and I have felt rewarded by many fine
comments through the years from people who have personally
told me how they have enjoyed my photography work and the
stories I have written.

On the title page: When I came to Salinas, California, about a
month afterwards in August 1955, I bought a local '27 "T"
Roadster pickup owned by Jack Horsley. It was a semi–basket
case, but I didn't mind. I was hot to get a Roadster that was
decent, and I didn't mind changing or adding to my taste. This
was a start, and it was great.

Also in this picture is my newly acquainted friend, Bob Walls.
He was doing a brake job on his just–acquired '40 Ford Coupe,
which he bought from Willie Wilde. Lavender paint was the "in"
thing in those days.

The red '55 T–Bird to the left is what I bought when I returned
home from Germany. It brought me to California.

On the contents page: February 1956: Here's Andy hamming it
up for the camera. Bob Walls is taking the picture, as you can see
by his shadow on the driveway.

This picture was taken of the Roadster as it was just finished
having body and repaint work done. The Hartnell College body
shop supplied the paint booth and area to work on the Roadster.
A '56 Ford "Glade Green" lacquer was chosen. Bob and I
worked together while I was learning how to spray paint.
Everything turned out pretty good!

Printed in Hong Kong

CONTENTS

Dedication

To my Father and Mother, in Memory.
Andrew S. Southard, Sr.
Mabel E. (Snyder) Southard
About Hot Rods and Customs,
"They didn't know—they couldn't understand."
"They understood—They cried with joy."
Similar words from Andy, Sr., to Andy, Jr., 1958.

And, of course, to Patty Southard, my Wife, my Buddy, and a Hot Rod and Custom Car fan. Thanks for all the support she has given me since we have been together for the past eleven years.

As with the *Custom Cars of the 1950s* book, Patty has come up with another fine poem—this time about Hot Rods.

Dedicated to Andy Southard

Welcome to Andy's World of "Hot Rods Of The Fifties,"
a pictorial review.
We hope you enjoy these selections
that he has made for you.

Andy has devoted much of his life to his photography,
he's known from coast to coast.
He's really fulfilled a lifelong dream
of what he enjoys the most.

Andy's not only my husband,
he's my legend, my hero, my friend.
Someone I can always count on,
someone on whom I can depend.

These pictures he now passes on to you
with so much joy and pride.
Read on my friends, and we certainly hope
you enjoy the contents inside.

With Much Love
Patty Southard
1–28–94

Here's Patty Southard getting into the 1950s spirit, wearing her purple and white "poodle" skirt outfit!

With clipboard in hand, she jots down ideas for her poem. Inspiration comes from looking at the gallery of Hot Rod pictures from Andy's collection on the garage walls.

Incidentally, with this posed picture, Patty is sitting on the front fender of the family car, a chop top 1940 Mercury Coupe.

Acknowledgments

First off, I would like to thank Tony Thacker, who introduced me to Motorbooks International by being a co–author on my first book, *Custom Cars of the 1950s*.

Through Tony, my twenty-five year dream of doing a book with my pictures became a reality.

Also, to Michael Dapper of Motorbooks, who was a big help and supported me to produce another colorful book, *Hot Rods of the 1950s*, I thank you.

Heartfelt thanks to all the people who enjoyed my first book and gave encouragement to do another book such as this! It's you, the reader and enthusiast, who has made this possible.

Throughout the many years of being associated with Hot Rods and Customs, it is difficult to name all the fine people I've been associated with to give credit where it is due. I must acknowledge my early years buddies and friends such as Willie Wilde (FL), Johnny Clegg (NY), Bill Acker (NY & FL), Martha Clegg Damone (NY), Elnora Clegg Houghton (NY), Ken Fleischmann (NY), and Bernard "Izzy" Davidson (NY), to name a few!

Much research has gone into this book identifying cars and naming people. Invaluable assistance was given by: Greg Sharp (CA), Rudy Perez (CA), Eddie and Mike Homen (CA), Dave Straub (NM), Bob Pavao (CA), Nick Reynal (CA), Bill Wainscott (CA), Mario San Paolo (CA), Steve San Paolo (CA), Tom San Paolo (CA), Harold Berg (NM), Bob Kraus (NY), Ray Smith (NY), Rudy Kershing (CA), Ray Soff (NJ), Henry Agostini (CA), Jack Horsley (CA), Cliff Inman (CA), Gary Shanrock (CA), Warren "Tut" Brown (CA), Jim Huston (CA), Bob Peverly (CA), Jerry Gaskill (CA), Ron Yetter (CA), Andy Brizio (CA), Mickey Sanders (CA), Ivan Scorsur (CA), Robert Duarte (CA), Dick Scritchfield (HI), John LaBelle (CA), Rod Powell (CA), Norm Grabowski (AR), Neil East (CO), Stephanie Harvey (CA), George Sein (CA), Dave Marasco (CA), Don Tognotti (CA), Don Tuttle (CA), Rick Perry (CA), Tommy The Greek (CA), Tom Cutino (CA), Mel Taormino (CA), and if I've forgotten anyone, you know who you are. Thank you.

Introduction

The first thing I must say is that all of the pictures in this book were taken by me in the 1950s and printed from my original negatives or my original color 35mm slides.

In some cases, I had to photograph an original picture of mine to obtain a negative to make reprints for this book.

There are a few pictures taken by other people, so noted as "Andy Southard Photo Collection/Courtesy of," used in conjunction with my pictures to make a complete point of interest or story. I thank them for their generosity.

The photographs in this book are what I saw through me eyes and through my camera lens. They were taken originally for my enjoyment and not for any historical record.

This is not a Hot Rod history, per se; it is the record of my times and what I love to photograph. Please treat it as such, and enjoy the photos and my personal experiences.

For those of you who haven't read my first book, *Custom Cars of The 1950s*, I'll give a little background of my early years.

I was born and raised in Oceanside, Long Island, New York. I went all through school there, and when I turned sixteen years old, I got my driver's license. At that time I was an avid car buff and had just started to learn about Hot Rods and Custom Cars. I think every teenager at that time was getting interested in cars—some liked Hot Rods, and some didn't! As you guessed, I liked both Hot Rods and Customs.

A few of my fellow classmates, Johnny Clegg and Willie Wilde, had some nice cars; Johnny, a '39 Mercury Coupe, and Willie, a '37 Ford Tudor Sedan. I had a '40 Mercury Coupe. We kind of clicked together and became buddies.

Many weekends were spent over at the Clegg house. "Ma Clegg" put on spaghetti feeds for all the local fellows, and everybody seemed to congregate there. We came to eat, have fun, and talk CARS! In my early years of learning about cars, I give a lot of credit to Johnny Clegg and Willie Wilde. They seemed to have a little more knowledge about the subject. They taught, and I learned!

About the same time, I took a photography class and was a member of the Oceanside High School Photography Club. What I learned there I put to use taking pictures of cars, something I loved at the time and love thoroughly today. At that time, I never realized how involved I would get in the subject of photographing cars and what my future would turn out to be.

I started out shooting pictures of Johnny and Willie working on their cars. I shot the processes of mechanical work and body work; I shot Willie Wilde chopping the top on his '32 channeled Coupe, out on the curb in front of the Clegg home. Ma Clegg even snapped a picture of Willie and myself, with his top cut, and roof on the front lawn. I was really giving Willie support, because I was just learning about body work, and I think Willie was also. It was during these early years that we went to the car shows that were sprouting up. One in particular was the Linden, New Jersey, show. It was pretty neat! We saw Roadsters, Coupes, some specialty cars—and I did take pictures.

Salinas, California, 1956. Another camera malfunction! I feel the picture is important, and I tried to print it the best I could. This is another salvaged picture.

This is the opposite side of the famous Mel's Drive–In, which appeared in my book *Custom Cars Of The 1950s*. In actuality, I liked to park on this side and get waited on, instead of the other side, which was always in the hot sun.

My buddy Willie Wilde was acting up beside my '27 "T" Roadster pickup. Becky Crabtree was sitting in the Roadster, laughing at his antics! There were not many pictures taken at Mel's. I wish I would have taken more, since I had many chances to do so.

Another of my friends, Bob Bales, belonged to the car on the far side of the Roadster, a lowered '49 Olds Coupe. I was parked on this side of Mel's in the Roadster when Mike Homen, president of the Slow–Pokes Car Club, came up to me, introduced himself, and asked me to put my Roadster in the 1956 Monterey Kar-Kapades Show, which I did.

I'm sad to say some of my early prints and negatives were lost through the years, and I have nothing to show for my efforts. Some of my early pictures and negatives I lost or misplaced because of my moves back and forth to California. However, I was lucky enough to borrow pictures of mine from Willie Wilde and Johnny Clegg; I copied these photos so I could use them for this book.

I'm glad I made those pictures for them years ago, because now a few are in this book. Getting hooked on photography was really great for me. I enjoyed it.

At that same time I was reading *Hot Rod Magazine* and thought it would be nice to be able to work for *Hot Rod* someday, photographing Hot Rods and Customs. That was always a big dream. Little did I know what was ahead!

I submitted two pictures of Willie Wilde's '32 Ford non–fendered Coupe to *Hot Rod*. One picture was with a model, Martha Clegg (Damone), who later married Jimmy Damone, popular singer Vic Damone's cousin. She was the first model to ever pose for me. I guess I was impressed with *Hot Rod's* "Parts With Appeal" page which always showed a pretty girl holding some kind of an automotive part.

Along with the pictures was a short article about Willie and his Coupe. I was hoping for the best and wanted to see both photos in print.

I kind of gave up, but in June of 1952, I received a check from Trend Inc., which published *Hot Rod*. I was thrilled with the ten dollars they sent me for Willie's article. Just couldn't wait to see it published. Boy, my first check from *Hot Rod Magazine*; that was really something! I was on cloud nine. As time went on, nothing appeared in the magazine. I didn't know which picture they were going to use.

Nothing happened until September of 1952, and I got another check—this time for five dollars. This was for that second picture, which was submitted for a future issue of *Hot Rod*. Needless to say, both pictures were never used. They must have gotten lost in the shuffle. I always kept my check stubs, because I valued them very much. Little did I realize that forty three years later I would publish one of the pictures that I had sent to *Hot Rod*. I really don't recall what I wrote about Willie's Coupe. It evades me right now. At least I can show you readers what that one picture was like that I was so proud of back in 1951.

Instead of going to college, I went to the New York Institute of Photography in New York City. A train ride from Long Island every day took me back and forth. I graduated with a Professional Photography Diploma in May of 1952. I was ready for the world.

That winter, with my friend Bill Acker, I decided to go to California to see the car show at the Pan Pacific Auditorium in Los Angeles. I also wanted to go to the famous Santa Ana Drag Strip, Barris Kustom Shop, Bell Auto Parts, and Bob's Drive–In in Burbank, all of which we managed to do!

The car show at Pan Pacific was terrific. I had the chance to see a few cars that I had previously seen in the magazines. In particular was Dick Flint's '29 Ford Roadster, which was featured in *Hot Rod*. At that time I was just taking pictures with black-and-white film. I was shooting with a 4x5 Speed Graphic (Press Camera) and was limited to the amount of pictures I could take due to the amount of film I had loaded into my film holders. I often think and ask myself why I didn't take more with me so I'd be better prepared. But, at least I took a few pictures which I'm presenting in this book which have never been published before. Really nostalgic for me; remember, I took these forty–three years ago!

The first time Bill Acker and I went to the Santa Ana Drags, we really enjoyed it. The only other time I had been to a drag strip was in New York at Curtis Field, an abandoned airport where Charles Lindbergh took off from to fly to Paris. But, I must say, the drags at Curtis Field were nothing like the Santa Ana Drags. Bill and I stayed all day. I shot a few black-and-white pictures, and I also took some

16mm home movies that I still have today. In doing the research for this book, I found out the first Santa Ana Drags opened at Orange County Airport on July 2, 1950. C.J. Hart, Frank Stillwell, and Creighton Hunter started the races.

In November of 1952, when we were there, Don Tuttle was the drag race announcer. The next day, Don put the results in the local paper where he worked. Through Don, I was able to identify a few cars.

It was also during this time at the drags that I took pictures of Lynn Yakel's fabulous '32 Ford chopped and channeled Coupe, which I had admired in *Hot Rod*.

After the drags that Sunday evening, we went to a local drive–in in Santa Ana. It was there that I saw that Monte Trone '33 Ford Coupe. Previously, it was featured in *Hot Rod* but was now under new ownership and painted yellow. I grabbed my loaded camera and shot a few pictures of it. This was the first time I ever shot night pictures at a drive–in restaurant, and it wouldn't be the last. My famous color night shot of Mel's Drive–In in Salinas, California, appeared in my first book, *Custom Cars of The 1950s*. Sadly, Mel's was torn down in 1973.

Bill and I went to many drive–ins while we were in the Los Angeles area. We ate at them quite often, and sometimes all the time. The most famous was Bob's in Burbank. We cruised the round drive–in and saw many fine cars drive through. It was like a car show all by itself! Bob's was a "must see" while we were there. In years to come, it would be where Norm Grabowski and his "Kookie–T" would be seen.

We stayed at Sherry's Motel in Hollywood during our visit. It was pretty much near the center of all the places where we wanted to go. The cars, the weather, the scenery, and the girls convinced me that someday I would become a Californian.

When we got back to New York, the '49 Ford Coupe that I had was changed to a mild Custom. The work of de–chroming the hood and the trunk, frenching the headlights, adding a '49 Oldsmobile grille, and spraying a metallic green paint job was handled by my buddy Johnny Clegg when he worked for C & M Auto Collision of Franklin Square.

During the beginning of 1953, the Korean War was going on, and I got drafted into the U.S. Army. Since the Korean War was declared over during the last two weeks of my basic training, I was sent to Germany for the duration of my two years in the service. As you will see later on in this book, I photographed a so-called classic '32 Ford Roadster in the town of Garmisch–Partenkirchen; this was the extent of my photography for the years between 1953 and 1955.

After the service, when I came home, I bought a '55 Ford Thunderbird. It was time for another adventure, so off I went to California! The T–Bird was packed tight as a drum.

My intention was to go to the Brooks Institute of Photography in Santa Barbara for their motion picture course; I wanted to get that piece of paper saying I was qualified to work in a movie studio. A friend of the family had connections with Paramount Studios, and everything looked very promising. However, when enrolling at the institute, I found out there was a nine–month waiting period before I could start classes.

So, in the mean time, I went to visit Willie Wilde, who was living in central California, at a place called Salinas. I had never heard of the place before, but found out the area was the salad bowl of the world because it had a lot of vegetable and produce companies. I also found out it had a lot of Hot Rods and Customs, too!

My chance in the movies ended with the friend of our family passing away, which meant my contact with Paramount Studios was gone. I did stay in Salinas for a while, having fun, working, and getting a Model "T" Roadster pickup that I fixed up and improved. Willie Wilde introduced me to Bob Walls, and we became pretty good buddies. Through them I met Jack Horsley, who sold me this basket case of a Roadster. Between Willie, Bob, and myself, the pickup turned out pretty nice, as you will see by the pictures in this book.

Salinas was great, and at the time, everybody was cruising Main Street and going to Mel's, the local drive–in. The town even had a drag strip! It was one of the first operating drag strips in California, open since December of 1949. Through the courtesy of Nick Reynal, I'm presenting a few pictures taken at the first drag races in Salinas.

The Salinas Hi–Timers, the Santa Cruz Cam Snappers, and the Seaside Slow Pokes were members of NCTA (Northern California Timing Association), and these clubs participated in the drags, which were held on the third Sunday of every month. When the cars ran, you could hear the engines revving up and the cars going down the strip—no matter where you were in town. It was quite sensational! Maybe the older people in town didn't care for it, the noise and all, but us younger folks loved it! As you go through the pages of this book, you will see some of the outstanding participants of the Salinas Drags from the mid–1950s.

Andy Southard Photo Collection/Courtesy of Stephanie Harvey

In the early- and mid-1950s, the drive–in restaurant was a big part of the Hot Rod and Custom Car scene. On Friday and Saturday nights, all the rodders seemed to congregate at the drive–ins. There was Bob's, Stan's, and Tiny Naylor's.

In the central and northern California area, Mel Weiss and family had a string of Mel's Drive–Ins. In Salinas, where I had lived most of my life, there was a Mel's. There was also one in San Jose, Berkeley, and Modesto; five were in the San Francisco area.

Interesting to see a Mel's menu from the mid-1950s. I can't believe the prices of the items! Can you imagine a cheeseburger for fifty cents, and a half of a spring chicken for one dollar and fifty cents! Ah, "the Good Old Days!"

Through my newly–acquired friend Bob Walls, I was invited to Walker's Cafe in Salinas where the Hi–Timers Club met and had their meetings. This is where I met Henry Agostini, Nick Reynal, Rudy and Carl Kershing, Bob Betzer, Charlie Alsberge, Vern Lacey, and Jack Horsley, to name a few. These fellows were all original members of the club whose existence lasted only five short years. After going to Walker's Cafe only a few times, a tragedy occurred; Walker's burned to the ground.

The drags were fun. I enjoyed going there, taking pictures, and, a few times, timing my "T" Roadster. It was turning 89 to 91mph. Not bad for a Street Roadster. I enjoyed driving the Roadster on the street, so I didn't want to get carried away and blow an engine. I didn't want to tear it apart and work on the Roadster all the time. I wanted to drive it and have fun—maybe a little street racing once in a while, but that's another story!

Once again, Bill Acker and I went to Los Angeles to see the Autorama at Pan Pacific, this time during the month of October in 1955. Three years had passed since we had been there, and this time I was photographing in color! Shooting colored slides and using a camera I bought in Germany, I had the opportunity to shoot a lot more with roll film. Only just learning to use color with flash, I didn't do that badly getting a half-way decent exposure and picture. As you can see in this book, I was able to capture the feeling of that colorful era, fancy paint jobs, pinstriping, and all!

Many of the cars shown here were featured in the leading magazines of their day, but the pictures were not in color. When color was used, it was just on the cover—not inside like they are today. This book gives you a chance to see how colorful the Rods were back then.

At the Autorama, one of the Rods that I liked was George Sein's Barris-built '32 Ford Coupe. It had the name of "The Flamer." Magazine articles showed the step–by–step building of this Coupe, from modified fenders to custom nerf bars to the custom grille in the '32 Ford radiator shell.

After getting in touch with George Sein, I found out that he saw an advertisement in the *Los Angeles Times* offering the car, in unmodified form, for sale. He related to me that he didn't have any insurance, so his father had to drive the car home when he bought it. He didn't even have the chance to be the first driver of his car. After a period of time, he fixed it up a little bit and then, later on, teamed up with George Barris, which is when it became "The Flamer." Painting and pinstriping was done by Dean Jeffries and Von Dutch, masters of their trades. After this show, I saw and photographed "The Flamer" twice more. It appeared at the 1956 Oakland Roadster Show and at the 1956 Monterey Kar-Kapades. I'm pleased to present those pictures in this book.

While I'm on the subject of car shows, another interesting thing happened to me concerning the 1956 Monterey Kar-Kapades. I was sitting in my '27 "T" Roadster pickup, with my friend Bob Walls, at the rear side of Mel's Drive–In, having a bite to eat, when a fellow by the name of Mike Homen came up to the Roadster and introduced himself. Mike was the president of the Slow Pokes Car Club from Seaside. He was pleased with the looks of my Roadster, and I was asked to bring it to the Kar-Kapades Show. Mike said, "I will pay you $15 to bring it to the show," and it was agreed upon. Can you imagine, $15 to go to a show in 1956? All I had to do was drive it about twenty miles to the show. I did get a trophy, for third place in my class. I was proud of that trophy and still have it.

The Slow Pokes Car Club was first organized in November of 1948 with thirteen members. Meetings were first held at a garage in Seaside, which is where they chose the name of the club as well as their emblem, the turtle. To be different, the name chosen for the first show was "Kustom Kar–Kapades." After the third year it just became "Kar–Kapades." Then, in 1962, it changed to "Kar–Kapades, Country Club of Car Shows." A fall show, called "Speedorama," was also started at that time.

Today, Mike Homen and I are fellow members of the honored Oakland Roadster Show Hall Of Fame group, an honor which was bestowed upon us for contributions through the years to the Oakland Roadster Show.

One memory of the shows that always comes to mind is when I met Blackie Gejeian at the Kar–Kapades in 1956. He was very cordial to me at that time, and we have been friends for many, many years.

When the show was over that Sunday night, Blackie started up his Roadster and slowly drove it out the double doors onto the entrance of the back green lawn. Trailers were parked to load up some of the show cars. Blackie, as spunky as he is, decided to rev up the "T" and do some slippin' and slidin' on the wet grass; he started to make figure eights with his Roadster. Just having a ball! Eventually, he straightened the Roadster out and headed straight for his trailer. Over the blaring sounds of exhaust pipes, I could hear Blackie laughing. The ramps were down, and I heard the "whoosh" as he drove it up onto the trailer. Blackie's laugh is so distinctive, and you know, I can still hear his laugh today, just as it was in 1956.

Since I have mentioned the Oakland Roadster Show and the Kar–Kapades of Monterey, I should mention some of the other shows that were also in existence at that time. I went to some of the other shows in those early days and regret not shooting pictures while I was there. Going to some of the shows was done on the spur of the moment, and I wasn't equipped with a camera to shoot pictures, which was unusual for me, because I was always ready to shoot pictures.

Some of the other outstanding shows were the San Mateo Car Show, the Turlock Motorcade, the San Jose Autorama, the Fresno Autorama, and the Bakersfield Car Show. It's hard to believe I didn't take pictures at some of these shows. At the time, I was just a spectator.

During the latter part of 1956, I headed back east again. Relatives and acquaintances used to kid with me, telling me I was a commuter going back and forth, west to east, east to west.

For a time, all I was doing for an occupation was pinstriping. I worked out of my parents' garage at home. Often cars were parked in the driveway, waiting to be striped. Weekends were busy, with two or three cars parked in line.

Business was good. My personal car was a mildly customized '56 Ford Victoria, a la California style! It was lowered in the front (raked cars with a slight forward tilt were popular), sported a molded hood with 114 louvers, had a modified stock grille, had the trunk de–chromed, used modified stock taillights, carried Douglas glass-packed mufflers which sounded very deep and mellow, and, of course, ran the new trend, chromed lakes plugs! I had the short ones coming out from under my front fender wells, running along the lower body panel up to about one third into the length on the driver door. This Victoria appeared on page twenty–eight of my *Custom Cars of the 1950s* book. As it was, my car was a rolling advertisement for my pinstriping talent.

There was a short period of time when I was doing some striping out of the Foreign Kustom Shop, on Jericho Turnpike in Huntington, Long Island, not far from where I lived. This is where I met shop owner and customizer, Eddie Eaton. I got the big job of pinstriping his '27 "T" Ford Competition Roadster pickup. A black-and-white picture appears in this book showing just what I did with his Roadster. It was a pretty wild stripe job for it's time!

Car shows were few on the East Coast, not like the plentiful shows in California. I did enter my '56 Ford Victoria in shows on Long Island. After I sold my Ford, I had a customized '55 Chevy (see page twenty–nine of my *Custom Cars of the 1950s* book) which I showed at the Hempstead Armory on Long Island. I also did pinstriping there; somebody took a picture of me striping, and it appeared in *Rodding and Restyling Magazine*, a New York-based magazine.

When I had my '58 Chevy, it too was customized, and I put it in the Rupp Chevrolet Dealership Car Show one weekend. These were fun times in New York, and a few cars from that show appear in this book.

The 1958 East Coast Round–Up Show was put on by the Drivin' Deuces Club at the Teaneck Armory in Teaneck, New Jersey. The club's '40 Ford pickup project car appeared there. It was through this show that I met Harry Bradley, the well–known, outstanding automotive artist and designer. Harry designed the "Drivin' Deuces" customized pickup, which is featured in this book.

Another famous car at that show was Jack Lentz's "Golden Rod" '32 Ford channeled Roadster. A very outstanding Roadster of the East Coast.

Eventually I did move back to California again and still live in Salinas. From the mid–1950s and into the 1960s, I lived in Salinas and in the Los Angeles areas of Anaheim and Glendale. I was very pleased and fortunate to have worked for Petersen Publishing Company in the capacity of managing editor of *Rod & Custom Magazine* in the early 1960s.

But now we are talking about the 1960s, and that's an era outside of what this book is all about. Maybe someday I'll have the opportunity to do a book on Hot Rods and Customs of the 1960s and present more brilliant color and black-and-white pictures, along with historical trivia and some personal experiences.

There are a few cars presented in this book that I could not identify by owner or where they were from. If anyone recognizes any of these, please feel free to write me to let me know who these owners are.

I hope you enjoy *Hot Rods of The 1950s*. Your thoughts and comments would be welcomed.

March, 1995
Andy Southard, Jr.
5 San Juan Drive
Salinas, California 93901
U.S.A.

I continued my pinstriping back in New York in the latter part of 1956. I worked out of my parents' garage, pinstriping Rods, Customs, stock type cars, and motorcycles.

Then, for a while, I was striping out of Foreign Kustom Shop, on East Jericho Turnpike in Huntington, Long Island. The shop was owned and operated by Eddie Eaton.

In this picture, I was striping Eddie's personal '27 "T" Competition Roadster pickup. The colors were white and brush gold. Here is a front close–up of the nosepiece's pinstriped pattern. My signature, "Andy '56," can be seen on the front nose section.

NEXT PAGES

Dave Dias' father–in–law gave him this '28 Ford Roadster pickup in the mid–'50s. A sheet metal worker from Concord, California, Dave knew what he wanted when he built his show-winning Roadster. The body was set back 6in; the bed was shortened to 3ft; extra length hood and side panels were made; the body work and paint was done by Byer Custom Painting of Rio Vista, California. The windshield was chopped 4in. 1931 Ford fenders with bobbed rears were used to match the shortened bed. Sixteen–inch, '39 Ford wheels were used in the rear— 15in Fords up front.

The engine was set back and ran a fan for cooling. The 342ci '49 Cadillac engine had an Edelbrock intake manifold that held three Stromberg 97 carbs.

In the early years, Dave was a member of the Bay Area Roadster Club and was there when I became a member.

Hot Rods of the 1950s

ABOVE

My high school buddy Willie Wilde bought this '32 Ford five–window Coupe from Ernie Evans in 1951. After a short time, Willie made some changes, more to his liking.

Snow tread tires in the rear were changed to regular tires. The '48 Mercury engine was modified with Edelbrock heads, dual carbs with velocity stacks, chrome oil filter and generator cover, a 3 5/16in bore with a 1/4in stroke, and an Iskenderian cam. The Coupe was blue originally, and at this time it was bronze.

My first model to pose with a Hot Rod was sixteen-year-old Martha Clegg (Damone). I was following the tradition of *Hot Rod Magazine*'s "Parts With Appeal" column, which appealed to me. Two pictures were sent to *Hot Rod* with a short story, paid for in 1952 but never used until now.

LEFT

Oceanside, Long Island, New York, 1951. For Willie Wilde, it was a busy year. He bought a '32 Ford five–window Coupe. I had to get into the picture also, so I had "Ma Clegg" operate the camera to capture Willie and myself. I am standing out in the street; Willie is inside taking measurements. I think the neighborhood people thought we were crazy, cutting the top off a car and lowering it down. They must have said, "Those crazy kids!" Once again, this is a salvaged picture by means of copying the original print. Willie was chopping the top on his Coupe; roof pieces and tops of doors were laying on the yard lawn. Hacksawing and cutting were done out by the street curb. Looks like total rejuvenation was in progress with the engine out.

ABOVE

My high school buddy Johnny Clegg bought a '32 Ford Coupe from another friend of ours, Bill Acker, in 1950. The first thing Johnny wanted to do was channel the body over the frame, which he did. Then came the task of removing the chicken wire, with the padding, etc., from the center of the roof. Then Johnny converted the top to an all steel roof. Johnny did this when he was working for C & M Auto Collision in Franklin Square, New York.

Other body modifications included filling in the cowl air vent, filling in the grille shell, and converting the rumble seat to a trunk lid. Striving for perfection, the body work was done three times, and it was also painted three times—Robin Egg Blue. The engine was a '51 Mercury with an Iskenderian 404 Jr. cam,

ported and polished; the manifold was an Edelbrock with three Holly carbs. The high compression heads were Osecki 9.1 with three water outlets on top. The Coupe turned 121mph at the Linden, New Jersey, Drags.

This last picture was taken in the Clegg driveway, with Johnny's sixteen–year–old sister, Lee "Tiny" Clegg (Houghton). This was the second gal to pose for me when I wanted to use a model with Johnny's car. She was a striking redhead with a marvelous figure! In November 1994, Johnny and his wife Elnora visited us here in California.

ABOVE

In November of 1952, my buddy Bill Acker and I left New York to head for California. While there, we had the pleasure of visiting Bell Auto Parts, where I bought the fender skirts for my '49 Ford, which is shown in the picture. Before we left, I had to walk across the street and shoot a picture of this famous speed shop. By the way, that's Bill sitting in my Ford, and get a load of the '33 Ford three–window Coupe to the right of the picture. It was a beauty ! I felt it "a must" to put this picture in this book, because it's historic nostalgia, which is the only way it can be described.

The place had it's start in 1923 when George Wight carried ordinary parts for the cars of that day. It wasn't very long before he carried used speed and power equipment. George assisted with organizing Muroc Dry Lakes meets and helped form the Southern California Timing Association (SCTA).

In 1937, Roy Richter set up a race car manufacturing shop at the rear of Wight's establishment. In 1943, George passed away. During the remaining years of World War II, Mrs. Wight kept the business going. At the end of the war, Roy bought out the business and had a full–scale operation. From that time on, Bell Auto Parts was the leader in the speed equipment field. They carried all the leading brand name speed equipment, from Weiand to Edelbrock; in the 1950's, their mailing list contained addresses of over 30,000 customers. That's a record in itself!

Lynn Yakel was from Montebello, California. This youngster had a chopped (3 1/2in) and channeled '32 Ford Coupe. Its Mercury engine was bored .060in over. The car boasted a chromed front dropped axle, custom hood and side panels with 132 louvers, and a '40 Ford rear end with 3.78 gears. The Coupe was clocked at 126mph. Originally painted maroon, the color had been changed to metallic Forest Green when I saw it at the Santa Ana Drag Strip in 1952. I was tickled to death that I could see the Rod in person and take a picture, as you see here.

This 1933 Ford "Cavalier" Coupe was built in Long Beach, California, by a father and son team, Ike and Monte Trone. The Trones did everything themselves, including engine work and chassis suspension, but Virgil Smith did the special race car nose. Monte was a member of the Cavalier's Car Club. The Coupe sported a Merc engine that was bored .060in over, stroked 1/4in, ported, relieved, and balanced. The heads were Edelbrock; the cam was by Winfield. A Burns manifold was on this 265ci engine.

One night after the drag races, we cruised into the town of Santa Ana and hit a few drive–ins. In one drive-in (of which I can't remember the name) came this '33 Ford Coupe. I recognized it right away as the Monte Trone Coupe, but this time it was cream colored. I stepped out and stopped the Coupe and asked the fellow behind the wheel to hold so I could shoot a few pictures. "OK," he said. I grabbed my 4x5 Press Speed Graphic and shot this front picture; I also photographed a three–quarters front shot. I thanked him, and he drove off. Never did get a chance to talk to him.

Three years later, I was sitting at Mel's Drive–In in Salinas, my home town, in my '27 "T" Roadster pickup (yellow at the time) when this neat black '53 Ford pulled up beside me. The two fellows in the car started talking with me about my Roadster. They liked it, our conversation was good, and we became friends. The two fellows were stationed at Fort Ord Army Base just seven miles from Salinas.

During the short period of time of knowing these guys, I showed them some of the pictures I had shot of Rods and Customs. Lo and behold, the one fellow, James Kilpatrick, shouted out, "It's me sitting in the Coupe!" Was it fate shooting the pictures at the Santa Ana drive–in, and then meeting and becoming friends with the same fellow?

Kilpatrick loved to race, which he did once too often, and, to make a long story short, rolled over his '53 Ford one evening into the lettuce fields of the Salinas Valley. The police came, and the ambulance arrived. James' arm was hurt, so they took him to the U.S. Army Hospital at Fort Ord, and I never saw or heard from him again.

ABOVE

November 1952, Pan Pacific
Auditorium, 3rd Annual
Autorama. Joe Rose, Inglewood,
California, displayed this bright red
'29 Ford Roadster body on a '32
Ford frame. Traditional in every
way, this car was non–fendered,
had cut down bobbed Model "A"
rear fenders, a molded cowl, a
chopped windshield slanted
backwards, and custom-made side
panels and top hood.

The interior was black-and-white
Naughahyde, the work was
performed by Jim McKinley. Body
and paint work was by Don Roberts.
Through my research, I couldn't find
the details of the engine,
transmission, or rear end, but no
doubt it was flathead powered.

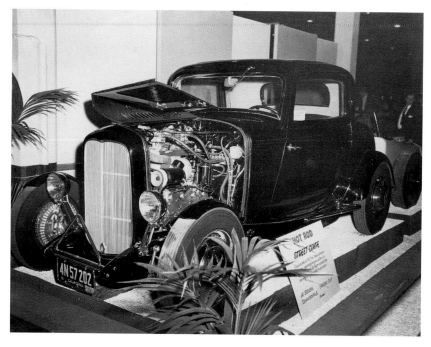

The 1952 L.A. Autorama. Herb Weigel's '32 Ford three-window Coupe was orange in color and could pass for a fine Street Coupe. In reality, it was a super contender with "Russetta Timing Association" in "C" class.

Running a flathead Mercury with Evans speed equipment, Herb turned 134.470mph in the mid–summer event at Dry Lakes. Seeing this Coupe impressed me very much.

LEFT

Once again the 1952 Autorama. Don Alpenfels and Al Brush of Gardena, California, displayed their beautiful 1932 Ford three–window "Hot Rod" Street Coupe.

Kinmount disc brakes stopped the Coupe, and power was by a 284ci supercharged flathead. The Coupe had a 180deg crankshaft, billet cam, magneto ignition, and four carburetors. The Coupe was painted a beautiful jet black.

Some years later, through my good friend Greg Sharp, a picture like this one was autographed by Don Alpenfels. Of course I printed another picture like this one for Greg. The dragster in the background is the famous "Bean Bandit" from San Diego.

ABOVE

Another 1952 beauty at Petersen's Autorama was Richard Nason's full-fendered '32 Ford Roadster. It was painted maroon. The sign in front said it had a big block Mercury flathead.

The body is basically stock, except for a chopped windshield and matching top, small sealed-beam headlights, and no door handles. Another fine example of a Los Angeles Street Roadster.

MAY 1952 25c

OVER **HALF-MILLION** COPIES
THIS ISSUE

HOT ROD
MAGAZINE

66% MORE HP
FOR OLDSMOBILE "88"
By Don Francisco

The first time I ever saw Dick Flint's '29 Ford Roadster was in the May 1952 issue of *Hot Rod*. It appeared on the cover in all of its red blazing color. I thought, "Wow, what a beautiful Roadster."

BELOW

Dick Flint built most of the Roadster himself, using a '40 Mercury V–8 with Edelbrock 9.1 heads, a Winfield 1 A cam, and three carbs. The nose piece, belly pans, and body work was done at Valley Customs of Burbank in 1952. Dick had custom nerf bars front and rear, with '39 Ford taillights integrated into the rear nerf bars. When stripped down for racing at the Lakes, it weighed only 1,900lb, with a speed of 143mph.

In the early sixties, I shot this color picture at the Hollywood Bowl during the Los Angeles Roadster Club Show. At that time, Duane Kofoed owned the Roadster. Today, the Roadster is being restored in Monterey, California.

I took this picture during the week of June 16, 1952; that's what the Kodak stamp said on the reverse of the picture. During this time, I met Larry and Gordon Gueffroy, twins, of Roslyn Heights, New York. That's Larry on the left and Gordon on the right, in front of their home. Ironically, they came from Palo Alto, California. Their father was in the military and had been transferred to New York.

chop top Coupe was silver/blue, with '39 Ford taillights, running a Ford flathead with two carbs. Johnny Clegg, Willie Wilde, and myself saw the twins quite often, but when we went into the service, we lost touch of them. That was the last time I saw them and their Coupe. Pretty nice Street Coupe for some nineteen–year–old kids!

BELOW

I am presenting this picture, because it represents the only so-called Hot Rod type car I photographed in 1954.
I took this picture of a '32 Ford Roadster in Garmisch–Partenkirchen while I was on leave from my military duties at Munich, Germany.
When I first saw the Roadster, I thought, "Boy, it would be a great start for a terrific Hot Rod." Imagine seeing a '32 Roadster in Germany! I couldn't believe it.

When I looked it over closely, I saw it had U.S. military license plates. To my recollection, the color was a drab silverish–blue. Peeking in the side panel louvers, I saw it had a Ford V–8 flathead motor, a stocker all the way!

Larry and Gordon's
'32 Ford

Salinas, California, 1955. At the end of August, I had the chance to photograph a pair of '32 Ford chopped Coupes. They were nearly identical. I often saw these two Coupes running around town, but I didn't know who owned either of them. Found out later who owned what!

This bright red Coupe, originally owned by Verne Lacey, sported a Studebaker engine and had '46 Chevy taillights (the other red '32 in town had Pontiac taillights).

When I took this picture, the Coupe was owned by Dick Shannon of Salinas, who worked at Industrial Machine Shop in town. When I recently talked with Dick, he told me he took out the Studebaker engine and put in a Ford 1/4 x 5/16 engine. It had a twenty–five tooth gear Lincoln side shift transmission, a '48 Ford rear end with 4.11 gear ratio, and '40 Ford hydraulic brakes.

During the time he owned the Coupe, he did some body work,

which was performed by my buddy Willie Wilde of "Wilde's Custom Shop." The Coupe was repainted blue with blue and white tuck-and-roll upholstery by Banning of Hollister. Come the year 1957, the Coupe was sold— not enough room for Shannon's expanded family. Incidentally, the other Coupe was owned by Dwayne Beetle, and it too ended up being painted Royal Blue. In time, it disappeared from town; I never saw it again. I wonder where they are today.

Andy Southard Photo Collection/Courtesy of Nick Reynal

In 1949, the Northern California Timing Association (NCTA) held the first Salinas Drag Races on the 6,000ft runway of the Salinas Municipal Airport. This was on December 10.

The Salinas 20–30 Club had approval for the use of the airport strip and invited local Roadster clubs to participate. During this time, the clubs that existed included Hi–Timers of Salinas, Slow Pokes, Inc. of Monterey, the Oakland Roadster Club, the San Francisco Ramblers, and the Santa Cruz Cam Snappers, to name a few.

Here is a picture of that very first day at Salinas, 1949. Sorry, Roadsters are unidentifiable, as are drivers and speed times.

Andy Southard Photo Collection/Courtesy of Nick Reynal

Salinas Drags, 1950. Nick Reynal is standing beside his '32 Ford chopped and channeled Competition Coupe. Chopped by Don Anderson of Salinas, this car was painted white with metallic brown scallops by Verne Lacey of Salinas.

The '48 Mercury engine had a bore and stroke of 3 7/16in x 4in; it was equipped with Evans pop–up pistons, heads, intake manifold with three carbs, and a Spaulding dual coil ignition. It had a '39 Ford transmission with Lincoln gears and a '48 Ford rear end with quick change. The Coupe ran around 103mph.

To the left of Nick is good friend Bob Ward, on leave from the U.S. Army at Fort Ord. The soldier standing in back of Nick's Coupe is Lynn Yakel, who owned the chopped and channeled Coupe appearing in this book; the pictures were taken at the 1952 Santa Ana Drags. Many years later, I had the honor of meeting Lynn and doing a personality article on him for *Street Rod Magazine*.

These are fine examples of club plaques I was familiar with in the mid- to late-1950s.

Top left, the early Slow Pokes of Seaside, California, club plaque. The plaque was of aluminum and was painted white with a stencil of different colors in the turtle with dual carbs.

Top right, the later version of the Slow Pokes plaque, which was a very heavy bronze cast. No maker's name on the reverse of the plaque.

Bottom left, the Hi–Timers plaque, cast aluminum, late 1940s.

They were a club from Salinas, California, belonging to NCTA. It had a profile of a '34 Ford Coupe, possibly replicating the Pierson Bros. Coupe that was a Bonneville winner.

Bottom right, the late '50s version of the famous Bay Area Roadster Club from central and northern California. This was my personal plaque, which I ran on my '29 Model "A" Roadster and on my '32 Ford Highboy Roadster. Maker's name on the back was Chicago Metal Craft, Port Chicago, California, a famous club plaque manufacturer.

Salinas Drags, about August or September of 1955. The beautiful drag '29 Ford Roadster was channeled with a chromed drop axle and front end, a custom hood with louvers, and a flathead engine with dual carburetion. This was sitting in the pit area, and was just right for me to shoot a picture.

LEFT

Driver is unidentified, but the Roadster was owned by Jack Hathaway of Santa Maria, California. Jack worked for a produce company and didn't have much time to work on the Roadster himself, so a buddy by the name of Larry Simas helped him out.

Unfortunately, Larry was killed in an automobile accident, and the Roadster wasn't finished. With the help of the terrific members of the Dragons Club of Santa Maria, the Roadster was finished and put in the Santa Barbara Fair Concourse d'Elegence as a tribute to Larry Simas. An outstanding club design graces the trunk of the Roadster as it prepares to go down the strip. My research did not tell me how fast the Roadster went.

ABOVE

Salinas Drag Strip, 1955. Steve San Paolo owned and drove his '31 Ford Competition Roadster. Steve bought the body in 1951, then put it on a '31 Ford frame. He boxed it and added a 3in dropped front axle, '39 Mercury brakes, a '39 Ford rear end with 4.44 gears, and a '39 Cad/LaSalle transmission.

The engine was a Mercury 3/8 x 3/8 in size, with a Potvin cam and a Weiand manifold with three 97 carbs. For it's day, 108mph in the quarter–mile was pretty good. Driv'nEat restaurants of Monterey and Salinas helped sponsor Steve. The Roadster ran from 1952 to

1959. After 1956, Steve went "sling–shot," moving the engine back and sitting in the trunk area. In 1956, running at Winters Drag Strip, Steve went 130mph. In 1958, at the Redding Strip, the Roadster turned 131.38mph. Would you believe that in 1961 he gave the Roadster away to a friend?

Steve, from Seaside, California, was a member of the Slow Pokes Car Club. While putting this book together, I had the pleasure of spending four hours with Steve talking about old times. Steve and his family reside in Salinas today.

The airport at Salinas, drag racing, 1955. This is just an overall shot that looked good to me of the pit area.

Just resting. That's what the fellow was doing by sitting on top of the Austin Bantam Coupe.

Another July 1955 picture taken at the Salinas Drags. Here is another unidentified photo. I could not find out who owned the Roadster or where it came from. The few times that I saw the Roadster at the Salinas Drags, I didn't take a picture of it until this shot.

The drags were over with. He was ready to leave and had the Roadster lined up to drive on his trailer. I motioned my hand for him to stop, which he did. Then I took the picture, and I never saw him again.

The Roadster is so beautiful that it deserves being in the book. By the

markings on the side panel, it looks like it was running in the "B" Street Roadster Class. Under the hood, he had a flathead Ford or Mercury engine with three carbs. Upholstery looks like tan Naugahyde. By the size of the steering wheel, I bet it's a '40 Ford. He took his hubcaps and windshield off, and he was ready to drag it out!

The year: 1955, the place: Salinas Drags. This yellow 1932 Ford chopped Competition Coupe belonged to Robert Rosen of Oakland, California. He was a member of the Hayward Head Hunters Club.

The body was channeled over the frame, the top was chopped, and the doors were affixed to stay closed, so entrance and exit was through the roof section. The Oldsmobile engine was moved back into the Coupe a total of 26in. The engine had a roller cam and an oversize bore; it had an estimated 300hp on gas. The running gear underneath was Ford.

ABOVE

Salinas Drags, 1955. The beautiful purple and blue '34 Ford Coupe was quite the contender, and was seen at the strip quite often. Art Balliet and Ted Gianinni of San Francisco, California, were the owners of this Competition Coupe, Broadmoor Service of Daly City, California. They were members of the Pacers Club of San Francisco.

The top has been chopped, and custom chrome nerf bars are in front. Paint was by Almont. I understand the Coupe was Ford flathead powered. Notice the hot dog stand to the right rear of the picture; looks like they were doing some business.

Ben Lupo of San Francisco, member of the Pacers Club of San Francisco, owned this flamed '29 Ford Roadster. Here he is shown at the 1955 Salinas Drags. The engine is a 3/8 x 3/8in Mercury flathead. The car has a quick change rear end and two–wheel disc brakes on the rear.

The Roadster attained the speed of 151mph at Bonneville in 1954. It went 126mph on fuel at the famous Saugas Drag Strip and 112mph on gas at the Lodi Strip. It also holds two class records at Lodi. Lupo holds two class records at Salinas in two meets. In ten meets they won thirteen trophies. At one time, Mario San Paolo of Salinas was a partner in the Roadster.

BELOW

Always enjoyed watching the drags. Here are pictures of the 1955 Salinas strip—I was viewing the cars in the pit area and taking pictures.

One car in particular that impressed me was Mickey Sanders' '31 Model "A" Roadster. Mickey was from Watsonville at the time, another Hot Rod community.

Mickey's Roadster sat nice; it had that typical "California rake," low in the front and not that high in the rear. It featured wide whitewall big and little tires with that salmon paint job (typical of that 50's era)!

The engine is a big 327ci '48 Mercury flathead. It had an Edelbrock four-carb intake manifold, Evans heads, a Weber F7 cam, and Edelbrock pistons with Grant rings. Hydraulic brakes and transmission are from a '39 Ford.

Its flawless body was accented by cream pinstriping. A stock Model "A" taillight is used. The rear end was from a '40 Ford and had 3.78 gears; it's not seen very well, but it was chrome. Also, there were custom–made rear nerf bars— chromed with an "S" for Mickey's last name. The girl in the background was Andy's drag strip date, Janet Bradley (Pisetti), of Salinas.

Salinas Drags, 1955. Rudy Heredia of Gilroy, California, owned this chopped and channeled '27 "T" Ford Coupe. The engine was a 303ci '49 Oldsmobile with dual carburetion. The transmission was a '39 Ford, with Lincoln Zephyr gears, coupled to a '39 Ford rear end. The hand-made outside headers went into a 4in tube alongside the frame and was chromed.

Rudy raced the "T" at the Salinas Drags and got a trophy for turning a speed of 97.6mph.

Rudy fashioned a different style front end than normal and used an early DeSoto grille. The top is white cloth, and the interior was done in red-and-white pleated Naugahyde upholstery by Banning of Gilroy, California.

In 1954 and 1955, the "T" was on a float for the Gilroy Bonanza Day Parade, a local festivity. In 1955, I looked at and drove the "T" when it was for sale. It was sold in 1956 to Buzz Sawyer of Watsonville. Little did I realize that years later Rudy and I would become good friends and fellow Bay Area Roadster members.

Drag racing in Salinas, 1955. Salinas Hi–Timers Club member Rudy Kershing owned this 1932 Austin Coupe. It was painted a brilliant red and yellow lacquer. The engine is a 235ci Wayne Chevy with Hilborn fuel injection and a Spaulding cam. It used alcohol and 50 percent nitro. Rudy turned the burning speed of 128mph in the quarter–mile.

At the Bonneville Salt Flats in 1954, Rudy was turning 154mph. I understand there weren't many colored pictures taken of the Coupe, so this colored shot of the Austin coming back on the return strip is rare and very unique.

A year later, the Coupe was in the Oakland Roadster Show with a new owner. It was repainted with a flamed pattern paint job.

I always looked forward to going to the Salinas Drag Strip, because I knew I would see new Rods each time. They came from all over the state. Such was the case of this typical '32 Ford five–window Coupe with a chopped top. Better yet, it was non–fendered.

Owner Bill "Wild Bill" Collier, who hailed from Santa Maria, was a member of the Dragons Club. Note the solid side panels on the Coupe. Unusual was the black painted frame and white painted body. The Coupe was powered by a 3/8 x 3/8in Ford flathead, with three Stromberg 97 carbs. Running time through the quarter–mile is not known.

Another Hot Rod that I know nothing about is this '27 Ford "T" Roadster. While on one of my travels in 1955, I was between the towns of Gilroy and San Martin. As I was traveling north on the main highway, I spotted this "T" driving down the road. Frantically, I waved the fellow down, and he pulled off on a side street, where I shot this picture of the Roadster.

We introduced ourselves (can't remember his name), and we talked at length about his Roadster, what was in the engine, etc. I remember it was a real "rump, rump" engine, so it must have been quite big. It had Edelbrock heads, four carbs, and a wild cam. The body was painted a metallic brown, and the interior was tan and brown.

I remember that we chatted for at least a half hour. He had to leave and tried to start it. I didn't think he was going to make it. Finally it fired up, and he waved good-bye as he was burning rubber down the street. I never saw him again.

ABOVE

During the later part of 1955, I used to go to the San Jose Drag Strip in San Jose, California. The drag strip could be readily seen from the 101 Highway going north (houses are there now), and one could even hear the cars racing on the strip from the 101 Highway.

Parked along the sidelines is Manuel Santos, of San Jose, with his '27 Model "T" Roadster pickup. It sported a stock '40 Ford V–8 and sat on a Model "A" frame. My research tells me that Manuel was the treasurer of the newly formed Jousters Club of San Jose.

The column shift goes to a '41 Ford transmission; rear end is a '37 Ford; and a '42 Ford radiator was cut down to fit under the Model "T" shell.

Manuel's brother did all the body and paint work—Pima Red in color. Wife Doreen did all the truck's interior in pleated black Naugahyde. A dropped '34 Ford axle and springs were used up front. To the left, Manuel is checking something in the pickup bed. The gals in the pickup are unidentified; maybe one of them is Doreen?

Once again at the San Jose Drag Strip, around 1955. I saw a beautiful '29 Ford Roadster on a '32 Ford frame. It was powered by a Ford V–8 with a Howard cam, a Harmon and Collins magneto, Edelbrock heads, a ported and relieved block, Jahns solid skirt pistons, a 22lb fly wheel, a 10in Chrysler pressure plate clutch, and a twenty–five tooth Zephyr transmission. The rear end was a '48 Ford with a 3.78 gear ratio. It also had a chromed dropped front axle, hand-made chromed outside type headers, and Pontiac taillights.

The Roadster took two "B" Class 260ci Cal–Neva Lake records. It went through the mile at 113.6mph and the half–mile at 111.3mph. All this is owned by Al Stanton, with the help of his brother, Leroy, from northern California. I recently found out Al passed away a few years ago.

San Jose Drag Strip, 1955. Besides watching the drags, I would go around the pit and parking areas to see what was there and take pictures. In the parking area was this beautiful full-fendered '32 Ford Roadster. Of course, I took a few pictures; here is one.

Little did I realize that Warren "Tut" Brown of San Jose was the owner, and that seven years later "Tut" and myself would be Bay Area Roadster Club members. When I recently talked to "Tut," I asked him all about the details of his Roadster.

Reggie Lotus of Los Gatos originally owned the Roadster. Reggie, I understand, raced at Muroc Dry Lakes in the early days.

"Tut" bought the Roadster in 1948 from Reggie and, of course, changed a few things to his liking, namely, installing a 3 3/8 x 1/4in Mercury flathead, with a Howard M–8 cam, Offenhauser heads, and an Offenhauser two-carb manifold. The transmission was a Lincoln, and the rear end is a '32 Ford with a 3.78 gear ratio. The

custom nerf bars, front and rear, were fabricated from Ford steering shafts. Minor body work was done, with the help of Gene Robeck, and the Roadster was painted Omaha Orange lacquer. Hall's of Oakland did the gray tuck-and-roll interior, white top, and spare tire cover.

The Roadster was re–done in 1949, and "Tut" showed it at the 1950 Oakland Roadster Show. I asked him if he got a trophy. His reply was, "No, wasn't that lucky!" Trophy or no trophy, it's a winner with me.

San Jose Drag Strip, 1955. Late afternoon, but still light enough to capture the beautiful American–La France Red '29 Ford Roadster pickup, built by Frank and Verge Bertuccio of Mountain View, California.

The Roadster won the first place class award at the Oakland Roadster Show in 1953. Power was supplied by a 250ci '48 Mercury engine with three carbs. The front end, steering gear, and hydraulic brakes are from a '41 Ford.

Interior is done in black Naugahyde, with a nicely fitted off–white top. Frank was a member of the San Jose Igniters Car Club. To the left is another beautiful black "T" Roadster pickup belonging to Ralph Appio of San Jose.

LEFT

After researching thoroughly through my entire slide collection, I must give space to a short-lived drag strip. The San Jose Drags were put on in cooperation with the San Jose Igniters Car Club.

I have given coverage of the Salinas Drags, so I must do so in fairness to the San Jose Drags. This picture was taken in August 1955. My early Salinas buddy, Bob Walls, "showed me the way to San Jose!" It was the third drag strip I ever attended.

During this time, the '55 Ford Thunderbirds were very popular. This photo, shot at the starting line, shows two T–Birds ready to drag! The maroon one to the left was slightly customized as I recall. The black one I don't know anything about. Who won? That I don't recall. In the background is a maroon '48 Ford pickup, owned by Babe's Muffler Shop of San Jose. Notice the casualness around the starting line. The girl to the left with the white shorts was the queen for the day. She awarded the trophies after the racing events were over. By the looks of the shadows on the ground, it was late afternoon, and the drags were close to closing.

ABOVE

Sometimes it gets very frustrating when I cannot find out anything on the cars I have photographed. This is one of those instances, but the Roadster is nice enough to publish !

The year is 1955, and I was at the San Jose Drag Strip. I was wandering around the pit area and came across this fine looking '32 Ford Highboy Roadster. Typical old-time-looking Street Roadster: red, non–fendered, louvered hood, chrome wheels, and black Naugahyde upholstery.

Isn't it a beauty? Does anybody out there know who belonged to this Roadster? Write to me, would you please?

1955, Pan Pacific
Auditorium, L.A. Autorama. The
Yeakel Brothers, automotive
dealers of Los Angeles, California,
sponsored this beautiful 1932
Ford-framed 1929 Ford Roadster
body Bonneville and drag strip car.

Built by Danny O'Brien, the
Roadster could accommodate any
of three types of engines: a 358ci
Cadillac, built by Lou Baney
(Yeakel Service Coordinator), a
292ci GMC six cylinder, owned
and modified by Yeakel tune–up
man Nick Arias, and a big
Mercury V– 8.

The Roadster was painted Iris Blue
with a fancy flame, and the
pinstriping and art work was done
by the master himself, Von Dutch.
The art work was accidentally
inverted by Dutch.

At the Bonneville Salt Flats, it was judged "Best Appearing Car and Crew," and it also turned the second fastest speed in "D" Roadster Class. The Roadster was capable of turning over 175mph at Bonneville and 134mph at the drag strip.

As you can see by the second picture here, a crew pickup truck holds many trophies won by the Yeakel Brothers Roadster. Incidentally, the fellow smiling for me on the left side of this picture is my buddy Bill Acker, a fellow New Yorker.

The 1955 L.A. Autorama had Bill Vogt's '29 Ford Roadster pickup there, but it's not a complete Roadster pickup! Bill discarded the pickup bed and shortened the frame to 87in, turning it into this interesting looking Hot Rod. Front axle was a Model "A," partially dropped, and the steering was from a '32 Ford. The engine was a '42 Mercury, bored to 3 5/16in, and sported a Howard M 12 cam, 8.5:1 Edelbrock heads, and a Weiand dual manifold with 97 carbs.

This second picture shows a custom-made gas tank, sitting atop a rear frame cross-member, '39 Ford taillights, housed in the body panel, Kinmount disc brakes, and a '40 Ford rear end with the drive shaft shortened 15in. Notice the '40 Ford steering wheel and red and white marble shift knob. It was painted '53 Buick Mandarin Red and pinstriped by the best, Von Dutch.

To Andy Southard Jr.

Von Dutch

In 1955, with my buddy Bill Acker, we went to see the L.A. Autorama.

At the time, this was the second show that Bill and I went to see together at Pan Pacific, the first being in 1952. The building hadn't changed much, but the cars had! The cars we saw had fancier paint jobs, light scallops, and much "fine line" pinstriping, which adorned the front, sides, and rear of the cars.

The striping fascinated me tremendously (not realizing that a year or so later I'd be striping cars myself and making a living at it)! The fronts of the cars had symmetrical designs— some simple, some lavish. Guess it all depended on how the owner wanted his car striped.

Thirty–one–year–old Kenneth Howard, also known as Von Dutch, was there, madly striping a blue '27 Studebaker touring car. There were stripes going every and each way—unbelievable! The crowd standing around watching Dutch stripe couldn't believe what they were seeing. "How could anybody put down such gorgeous lines, and all free hand?" It even amazed me at the time. I had the chance to meet Dutch, speak with him briefly, and then ask some questions about striping, which he graciously answered. Years later, one of the automotive magazines had a picture of what the Studebaker looked like after Dutch finished his weekend stripe job!

Von Dutch is not with us anymore; he passed away in 1993. Because he was such a striking figure, artisan, and well–renowned pinstriper, I wanted to share with you an autographed picture I have, which I highly prize. It's in keeping with the Hot Rod theme, since Dutch looks like he's striping a '34 Ford Roadster door.

The 1955 Los Angeles Autorama had a beautiful '32 Ford Coupe, owned by George Sein of Alhambra, California. It was fully customized by Barris Custom Shop, Lynwood, California. The Coupe was tagged "The Flamer" and was painted a rustic bronze metallic lacquer; it was flamed and pinstriped by Von Dutch and Dean Jeffries. Flames are a contrasting lime gold, with white, red, and yellow stripes.

The custom-made grille was of round horizontal bars. The Coupe sported nerf bars, front and rear, a dropped axle, hydraulic brakes, a completely chromed underside, a rolled back body pan with louvers, and Pontiac taillights. The running board pads are snap-on items for car shows.

BELOW

Engine compartment was filled up with a '53 Cadillac engine which had a Spaulding cam, solid lifters, and two four-throat carbs. The healthy 4 x 4 Caddy, built by George, won the Central Pacific Coast NHRA Regional Meet at 113mph. Notice the custom "Flamer" name under the Barris crest on the body panel.

ABOVE

The beautifully done interior was by Tom's Auto Trim Shop of Alhambra, California. The upholstery featured silver-corded black frieze cloth with rolled-and-pleated white Naugahyde, with carpets and pads to match. The dash held Stewart Warner gauges, with artistic pinstripes, and characteristic "monkeys" hanging off the pinstriping. Unusual and trendy at the time! Hanging from the dash is a fuel pressure pump. Window trim and door latches are among the few things chromed in the interior. Notice the custom white safety belts for driver and passenger.

Andy Southard Photo Collection/Courtesy of George Sein

How typically '50s can we get? George Sein went to Mark Keppel High School in Alhambra, California. The school newspaper, *The Aztec*, ran this picture on October 9, 1953. Dig the flattop haircut, the suede shoes, rolled cuffs on his Levi's, and the black-and-white checkered shirt. He was really hep!

The newspaper article said, "Keppel Kustom," by F. Gendian and J. Love. The bright red Coupe was a new addition to the school yard, and George was the owner. The story mentioned that it had hydraulic brakes and a louvered hood, a radiator cap that was inside, a grille shell that was peaked, and taillights that were tear–dropped. Interior was stock, but the paper noted that George planned a complete tuck-and-roll interior, with a nylon white top center piece. They said it had a 3/8 x 3/8in flathead, was Evans-equipped, had a Weber F–6 cam, was ported and relieved, and completely balanced. It sounded like the school was proud of George!

When I first saw Don Hentzell's Roadster, it was at the Pan Pacific Auditorium in 1955. At that time, Don was from Oakland, California. Working two and a half years, Don completed his 1927 Ford-bodied Roadster pickup. It had Model "A" front and rear fenders, an aluminum louvered hood and side panels, a '39 Ford front suspension with a dropped axle, and a Dodge Red Ram V–8 engine with Weiand intake manifold, four barrel carb, and Iskenderian cam.

At the time, Don was president of the East Bay Pickups Club and owned and operated Western Wheel and Rim Company in Oakland. It wasn't until 1958 that I met Don, when he put some chrome reversed wheels on my '58 Chevy Impala. Little did I know that we would become good pals four years later, both being members of the Bay Area Roadster Club.

In 1956, Don's best friend and famous fire engine pinstriper, Neil Hoegsberg, striped Don's Roadster pickup in black and gold leaf striping.

A few years ago, Don passed away in Sun City, Arizona. Notice the black Roadster in front of Don's; that's Norm Grabowski's before it became the famous "Kookie–Car" of television's "77 Sunset Strip."

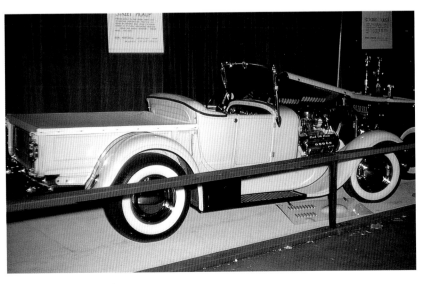

ABOVE

At the 1955 Los Angeles Autorama, I was impressed with Chuck Porter's 1949 Ford, chopped, channeled, and sectioned pickup truck. Painted a Golden Rod yellow, it sat with a few others from the Porter stable—a '32 Ford sedan delivery in the rear owned by Harold Rimer with a hopped-up Mercury engine, and a 1927 "T" Roadster in front owned by Tom Ruddy and Martin Weinstein. Check out the style of the time with the two fellows to the left. They're wearing the pegged "Peggers" pants—one blue and one white; I wonder if they were wearing blue suede shoes?

Chuck's pickup was very unique, because at that time there were not many chopped, channeled, and sectioned pickup trucks. So much work had been done to this truck that I would never have enough space for a caption to describe it all. The engine is a '53 Cadillac Max Balchowski re-work with an F–5 camshaft, 3 15/16in pistons, Howard pushrods, 4in stroke, and heads milled to 9.5:1 compression. I discovered that Chuck turned 105mph at the Santa Ana Drag Strip. For any of you who would like to read more details about the pickup, see the March 1955 issue of *Hot Rod Magazine*, as it also appeared on the cover.

Just recently, when I attended the Paso Robles outdoor car show in June of 1994, lo and behold, the Chuck Porter pickup was there. It's red now, as you can see, with a flamed paint job and no running boards. It's good to see the old-time truck is still around, and it brought back fond memories when I saw it.

56

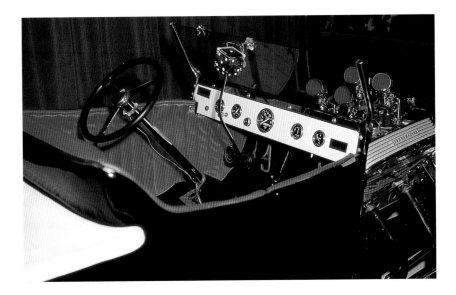

In 1955, Norman Grabowski, a twenty–two–year–old from Sunland, California, entered his black "T" Roadster pickup in the L.A. Autorama. This was the first time I saw his Rod in person, seeing it previously featured in the October issue of *Hot Rod Magazine*.

For some reason, at that time, I did not take any pictures of it overall, just an engine shot and an interior shot. The interior intrigued me—the bright red Naugahyde upholstery, the five Stewart Warner gauges on the dash, the modified '22 Dodge windshield frame, and the chromed steering shaft with a Bell Auto Parts steering wheel.

I just recently found out that John LaBelle is the proud owner of the Grabowski dice on the gear shift, compliments of Norm!

Los Angeles Autorama, 1955. Dave Marquez of Santa Paula, California, member of the Motor Monarchs of Ventura, displayed the '32 Ford frame. The Ford V–8 flathead was converted to an Ardun overhead valve operation. It had an under stock bore with a 4in stroke crankshaft, Hilborn fuel injection, Iskenderian No.2 camshaft, Smith pushrods, Edelbrock pistons, and Mercury rods. The 1936 Ford transmission has twenty–six tooth Lincoln Zephyr gears and an 11in Ford truck clutch. The rear end is a '41 Ford with 4.11 gears and a late model Halibrand quick change center section. It won "America's Most Beautiful Competition Roadster" at the Oakland Roadster Show.

CAR CRAFT

MARCH 1957 25c

HSL 536

ENGINE SWAP:
Buick V8 for
Studebakers
PAGE 16

AUTO SHOWS:
Special activity
for car clubs
PAGE 22

INTERVIEW:
The "King" of
car stripers
PAGE 38

LEFT

The March 1957 issue of *Car Craft Magazine* had these two gorgeous Roadsters on the cover; they were also featured. To the left is Dick MaCoy's '29 Ford Roadster pickup, and to the right is Dale Krutz's '27 "T" Roadster pickup.

RIGHT TOP

This classic pickup was at the 1955 L.A. Autorama. Dick MaCoy of Inglewood, California, owned this '29 Ford Roadster pickup. Don Roberts of Bear's Custom Shop in Inglewood did the body work and painted it Golden Rod yellow. The hood was louvered; the front bumper was from a '27 "T" Ford.

Trendy at the time were the chrome exhaust stacks coming out from between the body and the rear bed panel and running alongside the bed out past the tailgate. The canvas bed top was made by the famous Carson Top Shop. Under the hood sits a '48 Ford flathead with a Howard cam, Edelbrock heads, and an Edelbrock manifold. A bigger gas tank was installed under the rear bed. Also included were "traditional of it's time" wide whitewall tires!

RIGHT BOTTOM

The 1955 L.A. Autorama was in full swing when I captured this picture of "The West's Most Fabulous Dragster," driven by Art Chrisman of Chrisman's Garage of Compton, California.

Actually, the dragster was owned by Leroy Neumayer, and it was turned over to Art Chrisman and his brothers when LeRoy went into the U.S. Army.

The dragster is built around '28 Chevy frame rails. It included a Franklin steering system and front end and a Model "A" rear with Halibrand quick change. This picture shows the '51 Chrysler that had a Herbert cam and Hilborn fuel injection. When they ran the '49 Ford flathead, they attained record speeds of 154mph, which was pretty quick in the quarter–mile drags.

I guess I was at the right place at the right time! In the background, to the right in the blue pants, is Lincoln Cabraloff, who owned the channeled black '32 Ford Roadster. It was Ford-powered with three carbs, Edelbrock heads, and a Ford rear end. To the left of Lincoln is a young Wally Parks, editor of *Hot Rod Magazine*. I would officially be introduced to Wally while I worked for Petersen Publishing Company some eight years later when I became managing editor of *Rod & Custom Magazine*.

The 1955 Autorama in Los Angeles. One of the fine Street Roadsters on display was David Vincent's '29 Ford Roadster, from Maywood, California.

The Roadster was painted Fire Engine Red, had a chopped windshield, black-and-white diamond tufted upholstery, and covered running boards. The rear of the Roadster had elongated nerf bars made out of tubing and had '39 Ford taillights.

The engine was a 265ci Mercury, bored and stroked with a Clay Smith experimental cam. The block was fitted with Turner pistons; Eddie Meyer heads brought the compression up to 9.5:1, and the manifold had three Stromberg 97 carbs. Most unusual for its time were the Oldsmobile full wheel hubcaps, not usually run on a Roadster.

The L.A. Autorama of 1955. The famous "Glass Slipper" dragster was there. Painted a beautiful purple, it was driven by Ed Cortopassi and was built by Ed, his brother Roy, and Doug Butler of Sacramento, California.

The 1,235lb dragster ran a 274ci '46 Mercury flathead. The engine had a 3 5/16in bore and 4in stroke, Evans 8.1 heads, an Engle K–53–54 cam, an Edelbrock intake manifold with three 97 carbs converted for racing fuel, a Harmon and Collins magneto, and a 16lb Meanite flywheel.

The transmission was a '39 Ford using only second and high gears; the rear was a Halibrand quick change with 3.78 gears. At the Lodi Drag Strip, it turned top speeds of just under 130mph. At the Bonneville National Speed Trials, the dragster's best time was 181 mph. Not bad at all!

Fine line pinstriping was done by Dick Katayanagi of Sacramento, California, who just recently passed away.

Los Angeles Autorama, 1955. This beautiful 1927 Ford "T" Roadster pickup goes unidentified.

It was stock–bodied, except for the custom-made pickup bed done in wood. Interior was red-and-white Naugahyde, and the covering over the bed was white Naugahyde. By the looks of the four trophies and the "T" Timers Club Plaque, it must have won some races. Steering wheel with column shift looks like '46 Ford vintage.

In my extensive research, I did find a Custom Car with this club plaque, and the Custom came from Santa Monica, California. Did this Roadster come from there too?

L.A. Autorama, 1955 era. Once
again, a fine example of a Street
Rod Coupe. Bill Breece came all
the way from Ohio. His chopped
'32 Ford Coupe sported an
Oldsmobile engine with lots of
chrome, a Weber 3/4 grind cam,
an Edmunds dual quad manifold
with Olds carbs, and a Magspark
ignition. The car had a passionate
purple paint job. Aluminum
covers the running boards. The
front is lowered by a dropped axle.
Also included were 1954 Rambler
shocks, a '37 LaSalle transmission,
and a '48 Ford rear end.
What a wild interior for the color
it was. My research tells me the
interior was covered with
"Verslin."

The 1955 L.A. Autorama. This beautiful powder blue 1929 Ford Roadster, owned by Al and Bert Leithold of Riverside, California, shows it can be traditional and good looking.

Body and frame are stock Model "A," except for the Auburn center dash panel with Stewart Warner gauges, set in the natural finish ash panel. The interior is black pleated Naugahyde.

The mighty engine was a 302ci GMC with a 4in bore and a 4in stroke; it sported Edelbrock pistons, a Spaulding cam with a maximum horsepower grind, and a Howard five carburetor manifold. The ignition was from a Scintilla Vertex magneto.

The Roadster's best clocked time was at the 1955 Bonneville National Speed Trials, turning 127mph on alcohol. Twelve of the winning trophies sit in front of the Roadster.

Andy's pride and joy, a 1927 Ford non–fendered Hot Rod "T" Roadster pickup.

This picture shows the entire front end chromed including axle, spring, and wishbones. A special bracket held the license plate. Sealed-beam headlights were on the old style aluminum brackets, which could be bought at your local speed shop. Tubular shocks were mounted front and rear. Brakes were from a '40 Ford. A '32 Ford radiator grille and shell were sectioned by Willie Wilde, Wilde's Custom Shop of Gonzales, California. The engine

was a '48 Mercury which was bored .060in and used Jahns pistons. Camshaft is Iskenderian.

The 1007–B intake manifold was an Edelbrock with three 97 carbs. Other engine items included Offenhauser heads, a Crawford ignition, and dual point, dual coil Lincoln conversion.

The body sat on a Model "A" frame, unchanneled, with a stock wheelbase. The Roadster included a '40 Ford steering wheel, a column shift through a transmission containing twenty–six tooth Lincoln gears, and a 3.78 Ford rear end. The standard double

windshield was pieced together to make one big windshield. Big and little 15in tires were used—5.50 in front and 8.20 in the rear. Brand new beauty rings and hubcaps were bought at the time. Maroon-and-cream Naugahyde upholstery was used, with a maroon tarp over the pickup bed.

When I went back to New York in the latter part of 1956, the Roadster was sold in Anaheim, California, for the sum of $800. Another five years would go by before I owned another Roadster, which would be a Model "A."

This is the street where I lived, 140 Central Avenue, Salinas, California, in 1955.

Quite often I parked out on the street because I did not want to block the driveway, leaving passage for the landlord to get to his garages in the rear of the property.

One day my landlady, Mrs. Kubik, said to me, "Would you like to meet John, for I see he is home sitting on his front porch?" (the white house on the right, past the Ford station wagon, with the banister going up to the porch) I said, "John who?" Mrs. Kubik chuckled and said, "John is a famous author! Haven't you read any of his books?" Meekly, I replied, "No, what did he write?" I learned he wrote *East of Eden, The Pearl, Tortilla Flats,* and *Travels With Charley,* to name a few. I was interested, so we walked over to the porch. John was puffing on his pipe, and Mrs. Kubik introduced me to John Steinbeck. We talked briefly about Salinas, me being from New York, he having a home in Sag Harbor, New York. Fifteen minutes or so went by, we parted, and I never saw him again.

Ironically, my father and John shared the same birthdate, February 27. They both passed away the same year, 1968.

This is what always comes to mind when I see this picture, my Roadster and the Steinbeck home in the background.

In 1956, for a short period of time, I worked for Lloyd's Printing Service in Salinas. We printed stationery, brochures, and the Salinas Drag programs. While putting a program together, I saw that someone took a picture of the Steve San Paolo 1931 Competition Roadster. Standing along the strip edge in the background (circled) is a young Willie Wilde (left) and myself (right). So, of course, I had to make a copy of the picture for myself.

I don't know who took the picture, but I'm glad he did. To me, it's a historical record of how things were in the mid–'50s–it was fun! Notice how close everybody is standing to the starting line and the strip itself.

This picture captures drag racing history—in a split second!

The old Berardini Bros. Roadster as it was shown at the 1956 Oakland Roadster Show, under the ownership of Jean LaCoste of San Rafael, California, member of the Pacers Car Club of San Francisco.

This '32 Ford Highboy Roadster ran a '40 Mercury engine bored 3 3/8in x 4 1/8in, with an Iskenderian 404 cam, a four-carb manifold, and a Vertex magneto. The car had a stock '39 Ford transmission and rear end.

The Roadster holds records at Lodi, San Jose, and Salinas and holds the fastest time at San Jose of 111.66mph on pump gas with an elapsed time of 12.75. The flame painting and pinstriping was done by Von Dutch of Los Angeles. The Roadster appeared in the movie *The Blackboard Jungle.*

In 1956, Johnny Weston, of Richmond, California, entered his channeled '32 Ford Roadster in the Oakland Roadster Show. He was a member of the Elmwood Auto Club. After Johnny got out of the Navy, he reconstructed his Roadster to make it look as it is shown here.

The front end was completely chromed with a dropped front axle; the brakes were '40 Ford; it had a '34 Ford floor shift transmission with twenty–five tooth Lincoln Zephyr gears; the rear end was a 4.11:1 locked (no differential) rear. The upholstery was black-and-white Naugahyde. The stock dash was equipped with Stewart Warner gauges and a custom windshield frame with tinted glass. The car was painted Tropical Rose with black-and-white pinstriping by Tommy The Greek.

The Mercury engine had a 3 3/8in bore and 4 1/8in stroke, Stromberg 97 carbs on an Edelbrock manifold, an Iskenderian track cam, and Weiand heads. The Roadster clocked 100mph on gas at the Lodi Drag Strip.

RIGHT

The Oakland Roadster Show of 1956. In the foreground is Howard Hansel's '32 Ford Coupe. He was a member of The Ramblers of San Francisco. The Coupe was channeled over the frame eight inches, the front end had a dropped axle, and the engine was a '55 Cadillac. Also included was a Ford transmission and a Columbia overdrive unit. It sported dual purpose exhaust with competition outlets, a custom dash with Stewart Warner gauges, and a chrome built–in roll bar. It was painted cobalt metallic blue lacquer, with a baby blue-and-white Naugahyde interior. It took three years to build at an estimated cost of $1,700. Today, one couldn't even buy a '32 Ford Coupe for that amount of money.

In The Background

Joe Carlomagno of San Francisco owned the tan '32 Ford three-window Coupe and was also a member of The Ramblers Club. The top was chopped 3in with a filled roof. The engine was a 296ci Mercury and was connected to a Ford transmission and rear end. The engine had a Winfield cam and three carbs. The fenders are bobbed in the rear; modified cycle type fenders were used in front. The interior is tan leather, and the paint is Palomino Buff with baby blue-and-white pinstriping by Tommy The Greek. The dash is leather with Stewart Warner gauges, and the taillights are Pontiac. At the Winters Drag Strip, it turned 107mph. It hit 114mph at the Reno Lakes Meet. It was a 1954 California Class record holder.

NEXT PAGE TOP

One of the outstanding modified Competition '29 Ford Roadster pickups at the 1956 Oakland Roadster Show belonged to Robert Sletton of San Rafael, California. He was a member of the Marin Coupe and Roadster Club.

This attractive Roadster was painted Mandarin Red, and the upholstery was rust-and-ivory fabrilite. Modified with a bulldog front end and dropped axle, the body sat on a '32 Ford "Z–ed" frame. The engine was a '53 Olds with four 97 carbs and had chromed custom-made exhaust headers. Black-and-white pinstriping was done, no doubt, by Tommy The Greek.

To the right rear is the Marin Coupe and Roadster Club Crosley body on alloy rails. The car was constructed to use any V–8 or straight six engine furnished by various club members. It could accommodate several engines, including Merc, Cadillac, and Jaguar. Using a Merc engine, it turned 121mph at the drags. At Bonneville in 1952, it claimed the fastest Class C one–way run at 149.90mph and the Class B two–way record at 133.45mph.

NEXT PAGE BOTTOM

Oakland Roadster Show of 1956. Harry Love, Jr. from Redwood City, California, owned this chopped and raked '32 Ford Roadster which exemplifies the traditional "Highboy" look of the 1950s! Its paint included thirty coats of bright red lacquer by Pasodi's Body and Paint Shop. The front end was completely chromed with a dropped and filled axle. The car had a '34 Ford rear end and hydraulic brakes. The upholstery was red-and-white Naugahyde. The engine was a '48 Mercury 3 5/16in bore x 1/4in stroke and sported Edelbrock 9.1 heads and an Evans three-carb manifold. A '39 Ford transmission with twenty–six tooth Lincoln gears was used. A fine example of an "American Hot Rod."

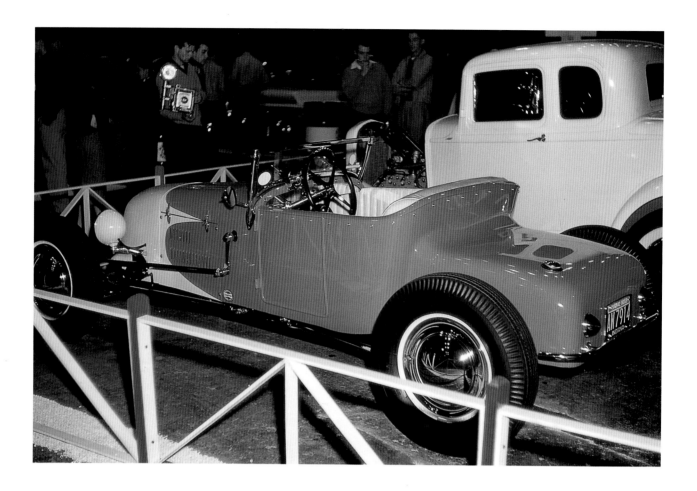

Oakland Roadster Show, 1956. I took this picture of Hoosier Hot Shot, Jerry McKenzie's '27 "T" Ford Special. It was built, with the exception of the "T" body, with a special deck, hood, and nose piece. Jerry was from Indianapolis, Indiana.

Jerry built his own turtle deck for the Roadster from the top of a '39 Dodge panel truck cab. Steering was a Ross unit. The front end had a '34 Ford front axle, spring, and perches. Other items included split '32 Ford radius rods, a special hand-formed nosepiece, and off-white pleated-and-rolled Naugahyde upholstery. The engine is a '51 Ford stroked Isky 1015 B track cam, with Edmunds 8.1 aluminum heads, and an Edelbrock manifold with dual carbs with "Belond" W type headers.

My research tells me it took a year and a half to build, and the Roadster was painted a reddish–brown color with yellow trim.

The fellow standing in the background holding my 4x5 Speed Graphic Camera is my buddy Bob Walls. He was sure a help holding my different cameras when I was shooting color or black-and-white pictures.

Oakland Roadster Show, 1956. Roger Hugo of San Francisco owned this '27 Ford Roadster body on a '32 Ford frame. The windshield was chopped; Bell brackets held King–Bee headlights; it had hand–made shock towers and a chopped '32 grille shell with a three–piece aluminum hood. Paint is Golden Rod Yellow, with accent pinstriping by Tommy The Greek. Upholstery is black-and-white Naugahyde; a full set of Stewart Warner gauges is in the dash.

Engine was a '49 Mercury with Offenhauser 9.1 heads and a three-carb manifold running a Potvin cam with a Vertex magneto. The engine block was ported and polished and was relieved by Douglas and Herndon Engineering of San Francisco. At the drags, it turned 109mph. Roger was a member of the Ramblers Club of San Francisco. Years later, my good friend Rudy Perez owned the Roadster.

The 1956 Oakland Roadster Show. The area in the foreground shows the interior of Harry Love's '32 Ford Roadster. Next is a belly tanker; to the left of that is Johnny Weston's channeled pink '32 Ford Roadster. To the rear is the 9ft trophy for America's Most Beautiful Roadster. To the left is Blackie Gejeian's "T" Roadster, and to the right is Ray Anderegg's yellow "T" Roadster. When I took this picture, I was standing on top of an oil drum that secured ropes to keep people from touching the cars.

ABOVE

NEXT PAGE

This picture shows the split winners of the 1955 America's Most Beautiful Roadster title. Blackie Gejeian's "T" is to the left, and Ray Anderegg's "T" is to the right.

Blackie hails from Fresno, California. The Roadster is flathead powered, and is either black or chrome-plated.

Every year the Oakland Roadster Show Hall of Fame Committee comes up with a commemorative felt poster honoring different cars or people that have been outstanding through the years in connection with the Oakland Roadster Show.

In 1993, they honored "The Flamer" Coupe, owned by George Sein and built by Barris Kustoms.

Others on the poster are the Alexander Brothers from Detroit, for their Custom Cars, and the legendary Von Dutch, represented by his famous flying eyeball.

I am privileged to have this poster, because I was inducted into the Oakland Roadster Show Hall of Fame four years ago and prize this highly.

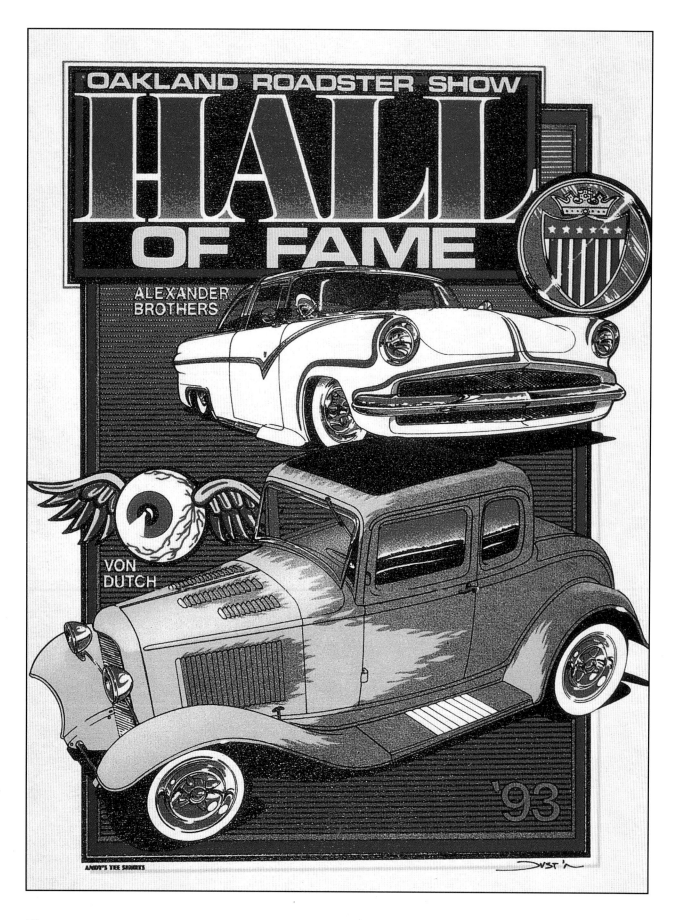

OAKLAND ROADSTER SHOW
HALL OF FAME

ALEXANDER BROTHERS

VON DUTCH

'93

ANDY'S TEE SHIRTS

Monterey Kar-Kapades, 1956. Originally, my '27 "T" Roadster pickup was placed in the main building, which pleased me very much. It sat right behind the Chic Cannon '32 Ford pickup truck.

With the early day shows, promoters were always moving the cars around. Needless to say, I was moved outside, in the patio area. I didn't mind because the Roadster looked good outside.

Notice the Union 76 oil drums used as stanchions to hold the ropes separating the cars from the spectators. The aisles were very small. Spectators' reach to the cars was easy. But this was back in the days when owners stood by their cars and talked with spectators when the show was in progress. This was the fun of a car show! Nowadays, you are not allowed behind the ropes by your car when the show is on. This is another salvaged picture.

BELOW

Monterey Kar-Kapades, 1956. President of the Slow–Pokes Car Club, Mike Homen, drives Bill Moore's channeled '32 Ford Roadster into the main building to set up for the weekend show.

Bill's '32 Roadster body is channeled 6in, and the radiator was chopped 6in to conform. The entire front end of the Roadster was chromed—axles, springs, and shocks. The upholstery was red-and-white pleated Naugahyde. Stewart Warner gauges were in the dash, and it sported a custom three-piece hood made by Jack Hageman. It had a '48 Mercury engine that had a 3 3/8in bore and 1/4in stroke crankshaft, a Weber cam, oversize Lincoln Zephyr valves, a Harmon & Collins ignition, and 225hp at 4,000rpm.

The buildings in the background are still there, but the trees are gone. My '56 Ford Victoria looks like it was undergoing some customizing work!

Through the years, I had the pleasure of photographing many of the Oakland Roadster Show's "America's Most Beautiful Roadster" title winners.

I even had the pleasure of photographing two of the winners for feature articles in *Rod & Custom Magazine*. I'm showing one of these now.

In 1956, Eddie Bosio won the title with his 1932 Ford Roadster, which in the early days of hot rodding was built by Vic Edelbrock, Sr. The timing plaque is still on the dash and reads, "11/16/41, Harper Lake, 121.45mph."

Bosio tagged the Roadster "Mr. Ed." Eddie Bosio lives in Daly City, California, which is next door to San Francisco. These photos have never been published before, but others, along with an article on the "Edelbrock" legend, have appeared in the April 1969 issue of *Rod & Custom Magazine*. Even though I took these pictures in 1969, it allows the younger generation to see an old–time Roadster preserved.

The entire front end was chromed. The custom windshield and frame held curved glass from a '58 Oldsmobile, and it sported stock chromed windshield posts. The engine was a 284ci flathead Mercury with all the Edelbrock accessories, heads, and intake manifold with three carbs. Chromed custom outside type headers were fabricated by Charles Tabusshi. Cliff Hadley of Burlingame did the black diamond button tuft Naugahyde upholstery. Added orange painting and white pinstriping was done by Tommy The Greek of Oakland.

ABOVE

Monterey Kar-Kapades, 1956. Tom San Paolo owned this '32 Ford three-window Coupe, which was parked outside on the lawn at night. Tom was also a Slow–Pokes member.

I learned from Tom that he bought his '32 Coupe in 1951 from Ernie Graveal, of Seaside Autowreckers, for just $100. Working diligently on the Coupe, it was completed in 1951, but just in primer. No paint as yet.

Tom did all the work himself. He built a 59 AB block with 3 1/4in bore and a 3 5/16in stroke, using a Potvin Eliminator cam, three Stromberg 97 carbs on a Sharp intake manifold, Sharp aluminum heads, and a Harmon & Collins magneto. The transmission was a '39 Ford with Lincoln Zephyr gears, and the rear end had a Halibrand quick change with 4.80 gear ratio.

The Coupe was pretty quick, attaining speeds of 123mph in the quarter–mile at the Salinas Drags, and later running 128mph at Lodi.

Tom also ran at other strips like Half Moon Bay and Fremont Drag Strip.

When I asked Tom who painted his Coupe, he replied, "I did!" I asked him if he painted it in his garage. He chuckled and said, "No, it was painted outside in the driveway." They just wetted down the driveway with water to hold down the dust and painted away. The aqua blue lacquer looked pretty good as I recall. The upholstery was aqua blue in diamond tuft pattern, which Tom did himself.

I also asked Tom, "What year did you sell your Coupe?" Again, he chuckled and replied, "In 1969 I just GAVE it to a guy, Bill Mason in Seaside, minus the running gear. He just got the frame and the body." Quite the era, wasn't it!

RIGHT

When I look at this picture now, I'm amazed at how they stacked the cars in the 1956 Monterey Kar-Kapades. This was the main building. Union 76 oil drums were used as stanchions; ropes were strung along the aisles to keep the spectators away from the cars.

Going down the aisle, from left to right, was John Anderson's '29 Ford Roadster, Dick Wesson's '32 Ford Roadster, an unidentified '32 Ford Coupe, Ivan Scorcers '32 Ford Roadster, and Chic Cannon's '32 Ford pickup truck.

Originally, my Roadster sat where Chic Cannon's pickup is; my Roadster was moved outside in the patio area. Notice how small the aisle was!

Andy Southard Photo Collection/Courtesy of Mike Homen

The 1956 Monterey Kar-Kapades was put on during the month of March, at the Monterey County Fairgrounds. Here is an overall picture of the second car show, put on by the Slow–Pokes Car Club of Seaside, California.

Look at the crammed main building. Car owners mingled and ate. The enlarged circle is of a young Mike Homen, president of the Slow–Pokes Car Club. It's been mentioned to me that they had fifty cars crammed in the main building alone.

The engine was a 260ci '49 Ford, with Sharp aluminum heads, a Howard M–8 cam, a Mallory ignition, and three carbs. Ivan Scorsur was president of the Santa Clara Timing Association and ran quite often at the San Jose Drags.

The black-and-white picture shows Ivan (right) cleaning and brother–in–law Hank Hopping (left) giving a helping hand.

Move–in day, Monterey Kar-Kapades, 1956. Ivan Scorsur from San Jose, California, took three years to build his '32 Ford channeled Roadster. He built it in a barn during the winter months when he was not farming.

The bottom of the channeled body had edges rolled under into a belly pan effect. The '32 Ford steering joins forces with a '38 Dodge front end, via a lowered steering arm. The '32 grille shell was shortened and shielded by a plate and club plaque.

RIGHT

This picture was taken set–up night at the 1956 Monterey Kar-Kapades. Dr. Frank Bonnet, of Saratoga, California, owned this beautiful channeled '34 Ford Coupe, metallic brown in color. It was powered by a Cadillac engine with a Howard F–5 cam. The Coupe clocked 103mph in the quarter–mile drags the first time out. Grille shell was from a '32 Ford.

The interior was white Naugahyde with brown inserts. The dash had ten Stewart Warner gauges. The Coupe had a Bell Auto Parts steering wheel and swing clutch and brake pedals. You might say, "This is what the doctor ordered!"

ABOVE

Monterey Kar-Kapades, 1956. The grassy knoll, in back of the main building, was set up with different displays. One was Mario San Paolo's dragster.

Originally, the body was on the "Bean Bandit's" dragster from San Diego, California. Mario and brother Steve built the special chassis from 2 1/2in chrome moly tubing in their Seaside, California, home. Body and belly pan were hand-formed aluminum.

The dragster's steering is a Franklin, mounted on aluminum hangers; the steering could be moved forward or backwards on the frame. The engine is a 59 A block flathead, 3 5/16in bore by 1/4in stroke. Cam was a

Potvin Eliminator. The engine sported a Weiand manifold, with three Stromberg 97 carbs, and Weiand heads. The car had racing slick tires, which were 16in.

Mario held records at Salinas, Lodi, and Bakersfield, turning a speed of 132mph. The congregation of people, left to right, were Bob Walls, California Highway Patrol Officer Petersen, Jerry Winnerberg, Mario San Paolo, and Les Bertelli. The Slow Pokes Car Club plaque was mounted on the rear of the bucket seat; a club jacket is on the ground. This picture was taken during move-in day of the show.

RIGHT TOP

Blackie started building this Roadster in 1945, taking eight years to complete. It won awards in Fresno, Oakland, Paso Robles, and in the Motorsports Show.

Body was trimmed 6in from the bottom and welded and molded to a 100in wheelbase '34 Ford frame. Custom-made cross-members, nerf bars, '34 Ford rear end, 296ci '46 Mercury engine, Isky 404 cam, Edelbrock manifold with four carbs, and a Harmon and Collins magneto were featured. The Roadster was all black or chromed and had a white engine block and upholstery. In later years, the Roadster burned, but as of this writing, Blackie says it will reappear at the 1999 Oakland Roadster Show Center Arena, the show's 50th Anniversary.

RIGHT BOTTOM

Rod & Custom Magazine called it "Blackie's Chickencoop," Car Craft Magazine called it "Shish Kebab Special," but I call it just plain fantastic and beautiful.

In 1955, in the first of two ties at the Oakland Roadster Show, Blackie Gejeian's '26 "T" shared the "America's Most Beautiful Roadster" title with Ray Anderegg's '27 "T" Roadster.

When I first saw Blackie's "T", it was at the '56 Oakland Roadster Show, where I took this interior shot. It had an all-white pleated Naugahyde upholstery (in 1954 it had black-and-white upholstery). The steering wheel was racing type, dash instruments were Stewart Warner, and only the lower half of the windshield was used. The gas tank was mounted in back of the "T" bucket on the chassis.

The full three-quarter front picture was taken at the Monterey Kar-Kapades in 1956, during set-up night. This is where I met Blackie, and we have been friends ever since.

Mountain View, California. Tom Peterson found his Roadster in a shed in 1950. After purchase, he started on the Rod right away. He stepped the frame 7 1/2in in the rear, dropped the axle in the front, installed 50/50 Monroe shocks and '41 Ford pickup spindles, and installed Kinmount disc brakes. The engine was a '52 Oldsmobile that was connected to a '39 Ford transmission via a Cragar adapter. The rear end was a Ford.

The body was channeled and included a custom hood and nosepiece. Fenders were made by Ray's Body Shop, in San Mateo, California. Ray also did the black lacquer paint. Cliff Hardley of San Mateo did the black Naugahyde interior. Exhaust headers and nerf bars were custom-made.

The Roadster was finished in 1959. In eighteen car shows, it received nineteen trophies. Sadly, in 1978, Tom passed away.

BELOW

The poplin shirt has the Hi–Timers script with an outlined profile of the Piersen Coupe. The Coupe profile displays NCTA (Northern California Timing Association), of which the Hi–Timers were affiliated. This was during the mid–years of the club.

Pictures courtesy of Robert A. Duarte of Salinas, California, an early member of the Hi–Timers Car Club of Salinas. Here are examples of the club jacket and poplin shirt.

Robert poses with the first jacket, satin in material, featuring a Hi–Timers script and a checkered flag with what looks like the Piersen Brothers Competition Coupe. After all these years, it still fits Robert and is in good shape.

I am proud to say that I still have the very first car show trophy I ever won.

I entered my '27 "T" Roadster pickup in the 1956 Monterey Kar-Kapades and was pleased when I received third place in my class; the trophy was only 10 1/2in tall. The lovely lady holding the torch is gold in color while the base is plastic and ivory in color.

LEFT

For a change of pace, we have Patty Southard posing with the last Hi–Timers jacket. This was a felt type jacket, popular during the 1950s.

In 1956, Willie Wilde was living in Gonzales, California. He was in the process of finishing his '27 "T" Roadster pickup.

In one of his trips back to California from New York, he took off a '32 Ford three-windowed Coupe body and replaced it with this Roadster pickup.

It had a dropped front axle, hydraulic brakes, and a stock Ford V–8 engine. The steering wheel was from a '40 Ford, and the car had a column shift. The body was in white primer at the time. Willie was starting his own business, known as Wilde's Custom Shop, in Gonzales. Willie did the body work on my '56 Ford Victoria and on my '27 "T" Roadster pickup.

Near the end of July in 1956, I took another trip back to New York. I jumped in my '56 Ford Victoria hardtop and headed East, via famous Route 66.

Coming off the mountain top heading into Albuquerque, New Mexico, the main route was right through town. As I came into town, I noticed a nice-looking '27 Model "T" Roadster pickup parked along the curb. As always, I had my 35mm camera with me, keeping it handy for occasions like this. I stopped and took this picture. Why I didn't shoot any more pictures, I can't explain. The picture was taken, and I was on my way.

Little did I realize that thirty–eight years later I would be pooling my resources to locate someone in Albuquerque who knew of the Roadster and could give me some information. I definitely wanted to use this picture in my book for it is a classic piece of that era! I went through three people before I found Dave Straub, who graciously got all the information I needed.

The pickup was bought in Los Angeles in 1955 by Joe Berg (who is now deceased), and it was originally painted green. Joe and some employees of Ace Auto Supply used a case of spray paint to get it the color it is in the photograph. Besides having a Ford flathead with dual carbs, not much else is known about the engine. Joe delivered parts in the Roadster all over Albuquerque. The pickup was sold in late 1956.

Ace Auto Supply was started in 1943 by Joe's father, Harold Berg. Ace Auto was the first to start stocking Hot Rod speed parts for the area. One of the main customers was "Pop" Unser, building engines for himself and sons Jerry, Bobby, and Al Unser, Sr. Ace Auto Supply went bankrupt in 1987.

Hartford, Connecticut, Autorama, 1956. Don Schoonmaker of New London, Connecticut, owned this '32 Ford five-window Coupe. The body was channeled over the frame, custom–made cycle fenders fit snugly over the tires, and the custom side panels had a moderate flame pattern.

Front wishbones were split and chrome-plated. Rear wheels were reversed, and the fronts were early stock Ford wheels. Dual carburetion can be seen, without a doubt, on a Ford flathead V–8 engine.

ABOVE

Autorama, Hartford, Connecticut, 1956. A fine array of Hot Rods with flathead engines.

In the foreground, looks like a '29 Ford Roadster had dual carbs on his flathead. In the center, the blue Roadster with the white top was a Coupe, originally. The body moldings give away the fact that it was once a Coupe. The dash is neat, with a few instruments. The car sports a '40 Ford steering wheel and a column shift. This also has a flathead engine with dual carbs.
The Coupe in the middle is Don Schoonmaker's of New London, Connecticut. This was flathead powered also.

In the background, the *Rod & Custom Magazine* "Dream Truck" was making its East Coast debut at the Hartford Show. It was at this show that I first met Spence Murray, who owned and showed the truck. To the right of the Dream Truck is Mudd Sharrigan's channeled '32 Ford Roadster, of Speedway Customs of Alston, Massachusetts.

LEFT

Joe Kizas presented the 7th Annual Hartford, Connecticut, Autorama in 1956. One show contender was Frederick L. Steel of Boxboro, Massachusetts. Painted a lavender purple, this '32 Ford Roadster was channeled the width of the frame, the windshield was chopped 4in, the firewall was chrome–plated, and it was said that Von Dutch did the pinstriping.

The front end had a dropped axle and a custom-lowered headlight bar—all chromed. The engine was a Ford flathead with four 97 carbs and lots of chrome. Upholstery was white Naugahyde, as was the matching chopped top. As of last year, Fred still had the Roadster, but it was up for sale.

RIGHT

In 1957, I went to the World Motorsport Show at the New York Coliseum in New York City. It was there that I saw Jim Wenstrup's '26 "T" Ford Roadster. Owning a "T" Roadster pickup a few years prior, my eye caught this burgundy beauty. It was built in Philadelphia, Pennsylvania.

With research, I found out it took eighteen months to build the Roadster. Taillights were '39 Ford teardrop, rear exhausts protruded through the lower rear body panel, custom chrome nerf bars adorned the rear, and the dashboard was chromed with eight Stewart Warner gauges. Chromed headers were designed and made by the owner.

The interior had rolled-and-pleated leather seats and fabric carpet on the floor. The engine was a Ford flathead, with dual carbs and Offenhauser aluminum heads. Custom front nerf bars supported the initial of Jim's last name. Notice the track Roadster style side nerf bars off of the '32 Ford frame near the rear tires. Truly a fine East Coast Hot Rod!

Andy Southard Photo
Collection/Courtesy of Ken
Fleischmann

Santa Ana Drag Strip, 1957. Hill
Alcala of Costa Mesa, California,
owned this "T" Roadster, which had
been a family project and family pet
for six years.

Old time looking it is, with a 296ci
'48 Merc flathead and a 3 3/8in x
1/4in bore and stroke. The engine
has three 97 carbs on an Evans
manifold, a Potvin 400 C 3 cam, big
valves, and Lincoln springs.

The tube front axle was from a '32
Plymouth; the transmission was a '39
Ford with Lincoln gears; the rear end
was a Model "A" with a Halibrand
center section running 3.78 gears or
3.94 ratio for the quarter–mile drags.

The Roadster speed is 130mph in the
quarter. By the way, the numbers on
the side were 00. When Dean Moon
himself painted the double 0's with
eyeballs, they became the first "Moon
Eyes," as told to me by Don Tuttle.

Andy Southard
Photo
Collection/Courtesy of
Don Tuttle

Just before my book was
finished, I received a
transfer decal from Don
Tuttle. Don was the
announcer for the Santa
Ana Drags, and he helped
me identify many
competition cars.

This decal is a reproduction
of the poster that advertised the
Santa Ana Drags held every
Sunday at the Orange County
Airport.

Andy Southard Photo Collection/Courtesy of Ken Fleischmann

Orange County Airport, Santa Ana Drags, 1957. Walt and Bud Nicholls built this dragster with the facilities of Quincy Automotive in Santa Monica, California.

They used a '55 Oldsmobile engine with an Engle 116 flat tappet cam, Engle lifters and adjustable pushrods, Venolia flat top pistons with Grant rings, a Hilborn fuel injection (nitro–alcohol fuel mix), and a Joe Hunt-converted Vertex magneto.

Bore is 3 15/16in and stroke is 3 13/16in. 10.1 compression heads were used. Estimated power was 425hp.

A '53 Healey steering system operated through a reinforced double tube drag link; the front axle was a '37 Ford tube type; brakes were on the rear only; a Halibrand rear end with a 3.43 ratio was used on most runs; the rear axle housings bolted rigidly to the tube frame. No drive shaft was used since the '41 Cadillac gearbox (second and high gear only) backed right up to the rear end. The best top speed in the quarter was 148.02mph.

Andy Southard Photo
Collection/Courtesy of Ken
Fleischmann

Santa Ana Drag Strip, 1957. Late
afternoon and the sun is going
down. Palmer Hamblin is the
starter. He's watching them closely;
any minute he will be flagging them
off to a start. Number forty–four,
the Roadster to the left, is a '32
Ford, and it looks like the Roadster
on the right is a '29 Model "A!" I
wonder who won the race?

Just like the drags in Salinas; look
how close the spectators are to the
strip and the starting line. Check out
the fairly new pickups at the starting
line. The drags today will never be
like they used to be!

Andy Southard Photo
Collection/Courtesy of Ken
Fleischmann

You say you have a date! It's
Sunday afternoon! Let's say we go
to the drag races! Drag races were
very popular in 1957. In 1957,
some high speeds were attained
with dragsters going over 150mph.
You called your buddy. "Hey Joe,
dig out your Roadster and grab
your gal. Let's go to the drags!"

Your Roadster is tomato red in
color; you're sitting on the
sidelines watching the drags.
Across from you is your girlfriend.
You slide over to her side of the
seat and give her a little hug and,
maybe, a little kiss.

Joe and his black '32 Ford
Roadster is sitting next to yours.
He's pretty hep for the times, with
spun aluminum "moon" discs on
his wheels. Joe and his girl are
sitting on the running board,
watching the drags too! To the
right in the picture is a brand new
'57 Chevy Tudor Sedan.

RIGHT BOTTOM

Besides taking your girl to the
drags, you also participate. A
number is on your door, and
you're ready to go! You're at the
starting line; looks like you're
going to race a '40 standard Ford
Coupe. C.J. Hart is the starter;
he's just about ready to flag you
off! (Notice he's not wearing a
helmet in the Roadster.) To the
lower right of the picture is Palmer
Hamblin in the white shirt,
another starter of the Santa Ana
Drags. Gee, I wonder if the
Roadster won the race?

The Long Beach Car Show in July, 1958, had this Candy Lipstick Red '26 Ford Model "T" Roadster pickup, owned by Al Neblett. The radiator shell is beautifully chrome–plated with expanded metal in the front of the radiator. The stock hood and side panels were chrome-plated first, then painted, but the louvers on the side panels were taped so the chrome would show when the tape was taken off. Firestone whitewall tires were on the '50 Mercury wheels with original hubcaps. The engine was a '57 Chevy Corvette, sporting a roller cam and two four–throat carbs. The transmission was a '40 Ford pickup with Lincoln Zephyr gears, and the rear end was Ford with 4.44 gears.

RIGHT TOP

The windshield was stock height with chrome frames. The dash was made out of mahogany, and the instruments were '56 DeSoto. The steering column was chromed, and it had a '38 Willys steering box and shaft. The steering wheel was stock "T." Upholstery was white Naugahyde, done by Joe's Auto Top in Napa, California. Rugs were red nylon, trimmed in white.

RIGHT BOTTOM

The pickup bed has a mahogany floor with chrome tie down strips. The tarp was white pleated Naugahyde. All body rivets were replaced with chrome flathead bolts. Underneath, the fenders were painted metallic gold. The entire undercarriage was chromed. Brakes all around were Lincoln. In four shows, it had taken five trophies—from First Place to Most Outstanding Rod.

ABOVE

Ed Roth, "The Pinstriper" from Maywood, California, owned this 1930 Ford Tudor Sedan. It was shown at the Long Beach Autorama in July 1958.

It was painted a bright red enamel and was scalloped in black, silver, and gray with white striping—all by Roth himself. The black-and-white Naugahyde top and interior was done by Martinez Upholstery in Bell, California. A '32 Ford grille and shell was used.

The front end had a 3in dropped axle and '48 Ford brakes; the engine was a 50 Oldsmobile with dual carbs. Notice the heavily pinstriped firewall!

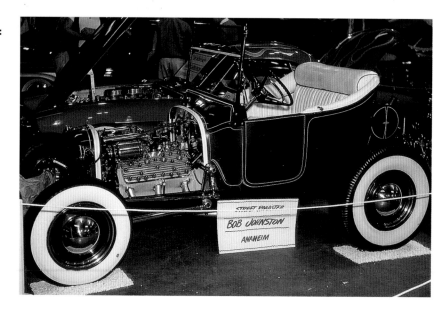

The Long Beach Car Show, July 1958. Many beautiful Rods. One in particular was Bob Johnston's '23 Ford "T" Bucket, named "Tweedy Pie." The name was put on the rear gas tank, and I was fortunate enough to watch Ed Roth put the name on at the show. His nimble fingers and his flexible brush did the name in a matter of a few minutes. The pinstriping was done previously by Roth.

The body and frame were painted Royal Metallic Purple. Interior was white Naugahyde with purple trim done by Golden Needle Custom Trim Shop in Garden Grove, California. The engine was a '48 Mercury 1/4in x 5/16in stroke and bore, sporting Navarro heads with dual carbs. Grille over radiator was a cut down '34 Ford truck. The "T" sat on a shortened '32 Ford frame with a wheelbase of 84in; total weight of the Roadster was 1,470lb. Bob was a member of the Orange County Igniters Car Club.

ABOVE

Two brothers, Dick and George Collins, from Whittier, California, owned this Pearl White '32 Ford Coupe. Immaculate in every way, and I was intrigued with the flame type painting and the open side hood. You can see the '56 Olds engine with four carbs.

Contrasting painted 15in wheels with baldy hubcaps and beauty rings gave it the old time style, along with Firestone tires and '48 Ford brakes.

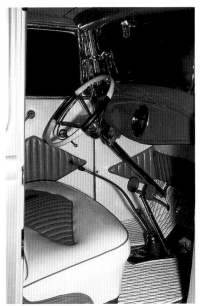

LEFT

My research tells me that Dick Collins, an upholsterer by trade, did the interior and trunk in white-and-turquoise Naugahyde. The steering wheel was a dished '56 Ford. Looks like the gauges in the center of the dash were from an enclosed unit from a '50 Ford. These pictures were taken at the Long Beach Show of 1958.

Tony LaMesa of Los Angeles has been a Hot Rodder for twenty-three years, and he spent four years building this "Original American Sports Car," as he calls it. A member of the Los Angeles Roadster Club, here's Tony's Roadster in the Long Beach Show of 1958.

The engine was a stock '56 Chevy Corvette. The clutch assembly was a '50 Merc, and the transmission had twenty–six tooth Lincoln Zephyr gears. Brakes were from a

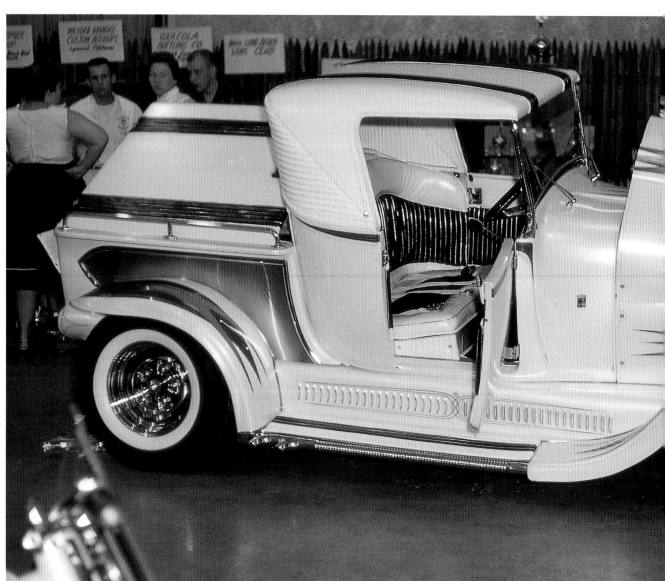

'48 Lincoln, and spindles and steering were from a '40 Ford.

The body had been channeled over the frame 5 1/2in. Notice the door hinges were molded and had fade–a–ways into the body. The interior was done in pearl white Naugahyde; the dash was a custom–fitted '40 Ford. The steering wheel and column shift was also '40 Ford. Tony's Roadster has been seen on the Ozzie and Harriet television series and in many movies.

LEFT

The July 1958 Long Beach Car Show was outstanding in every way! Barris Kustom's "The Ala Kart," owned by Richard Peters of Fresno, California, was there.

They started with a '29 Ford Roadster pickup body and grafted the rear part of a '27 "T" body to the front of it. The bed was completely hand-formed and fitted with custom trim. Modified fenders had 1/2in round rod edges. The fenders were scalloped in purple and gold underneath as well as on top. The luscious interior was done in black-and-white Naugahyde. Louvers were on the splash panels, and the custom exhaust went through cutout sections of the running boards. Paint included thirty coats of Swedish pearl paint, and pinstripes were done by Jeffries.

ABOVE

The entire front end was chromed and included a dropped axle, special coil springs with air lifts, and a custom front nosepiece that used gold-dyed clear catalyst rods to create the grille. Imperial four–way headlights were fabricated into the grille shell, and the car sported custom nerf bars. The engine was a '54 Dodge with Hilborn fuel injection and Vertex magneto. The Roadster won the coveted title of "America's Most Beautiful Roadster" at the Oakland Roadster Show in 1958 and 1959. The Roadster today is stored in Arizona—in pieces!

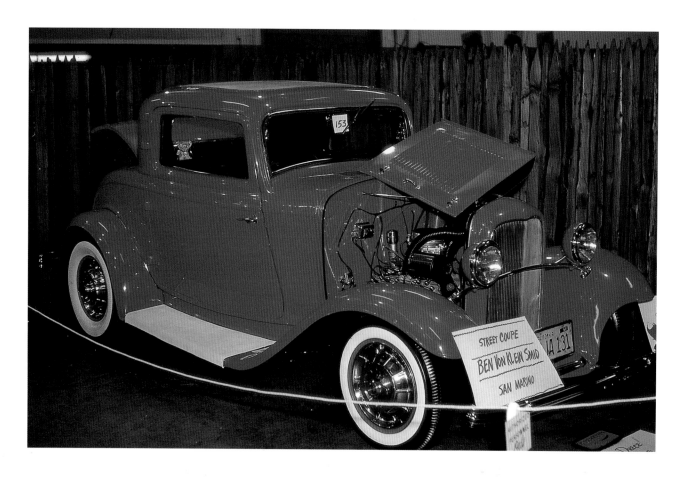

ABOVE

Once again, the Long Beach Show of 1958. This '32 Ford three-window Coupe belonged to Ben Von Kleinsmid of San Marino, California. This is Ben's first car, and hot rodding was introduced to Ben by his brother.

Can you imagine, Ben paid $200 for the Coupe. He then spent another $1,000 to get it in the shape as shown here. The body was painted Toreador Red while the interior is done in black-and-red Naugahyde. The '32 dashboard had a Stewart Warner panel with five S & W gauges. The front end was lowered by a 3in dropped axle.

Power was supplied by a '48 Mercury with Offenhauser heads, Edelbrock manifold, H & C cam, and a chopped flywheel. The insert in the top was made of white Naugahyde, as were the running board covers.

Members of the Long Beach Car Club called The Renegades appeared at the 1958 Long Beach Car Show. Among them was Ed Cousins with his metallic maroon '32 Ford pickup truck. The pickup was powered by a '48 Mercury engine with three carbs and Evans heads.

Body modifications included a 3in chopped top, a shortened pickup bed, and DeSoto/Plymouth ripple–type bumpers. The front was lowered with a dropped axle;

the interior was white Naugahyde trimmed with black piping. The steering wheel is a dished type, and the dash has an array of S & W gauges.

Chromed exhaust stuck out of the rear portion of the running boards while running boards were covered with white Naugahyde. Orange pinstriping on edges of scallops was the style of the day back in 1958. As you can see with his trophies, Ed did well in the car shows.

Also in July of 1958, at Marty's Custom Shop. Parked across the street, in a vacant lot, was Marty Moore's '40 Ford pickup truck. What a beauty, with it's titian red lacquer paint job, chromed running boards, wide whitewall tires, and chromed disk hubcaps. The bed has a white tarp with mahogany wood underneath. Interior was done by Kizer's Upholstery of San Diego in complimentary red Naugahyde. The dash was painted a matching titian red lacquer. The truck had a '56 Chevy Corvette engine. Lowness of truck was achieved by a dropped axle and dearched springs.

While visiting Marty's Custom Shop in San Diego, I saw this mandarin red '29 Ford Roadster outside the shop. Paul Bos of El Cajon is the owner. Stock body, but underneath the hood was a 283 Chevy with a Duntov cam and an Edelbrock manifold with three carbs. The transmission was '39 Ford, brakes were '40, steering was a '56 Ford pickup, and the rear end was '40 Ford with 4.44 gears. Front suspension was '32 Ford. Paul admitted it cost $3,000 to build, and this was his sixth Street Rod.

Andy Southard Photo Collection/Courtesy of Ken Fleischmann

I've had people ask me, "Andy, with all your pictures, how come you don't have any with your camera in hand taking a picture?" Well, here's one! Even though it's a Street Custom and not a Hot Rod, I feel it's rare to have a picture of me, at the early age of twenty–five, with camera in hand. I just took a picture of the front of this '56 Chevy and was going to the back to shoot the rear shot.

My camera is a 35mm German Leica. I bought it in Germany in 1953, when I was in the Army stationed in Munich. The camera has literally taken thousands of colored slides! Many of the colored pictures in this book were taken with my Leica camera.

When Ken took this picture, it was in July of 1958. We were either going to or coming from the Long Beach Car Show. Enroute, we saw this Chevy parked on the street. Of course, we had to stop and take pictures. So, readers, even though it's a Custom, it warrants being in the book because of Yours Truly in the picture!

Marty's fine little pickup was featured on the cover of the May 1959 issue of *Car Craft Magazine*. Also on the cover was a '27 "T" Roadster pickup, in yellow, which belonged to a fellow Bay Area Roadster member and good friend, Don Hentzell.

July 1958. Ken Fleischmann, Bernard "Izzy" Davidson, and myself went to Burbank, California. We were going to Bob's Drive-In for lunch.

Along the way, we went past the famous Andrews & Evans Custom Car and Hot Rod used car lot. Dick Jackson's T–Bird was on the lot; also there was this neat '29 Ford Roadster pickup. Unusual, because it was non–fendered! Traditional, old style! Not many Roadster pickups were seen without fenders.

The Roadster was nicely put together, with a dropped chromed axle and black Naugahyde upholstery. The sign on the windshield said, "Two Port 'Riley.'" Indeed, there was a four banger in the Roadster!

The price on the Roadster I don't remember. It most likely was reasonable, for Hot Rods were not big-dollar cars like they are today!

ABOVE

Another July 1958 photo, taken in San Diego. We spotted a Hot Rod for sale in a car lot, as the sign pointed out on the rear quarter window. The '32 Ford Coupe was channeled over the frame, and I believe it had an Oldsmobile engine in it.

If memory serves me right, it had an $850 price tag. My buddies right to left, are: Ken Fleischmann, Bernard "Izzy" Davidson, and Bob Haines, of El Cajon, California. They were looking over the Coupe. Wonder if it ever sold?

When in Monterey, California, I usually got gas at the Van Deusen Union 76 station on Fremont Street. One day in August 1958, I gassed up and took a picture of the '34 Ford Competition Coupe that LaVier Van Deusen owned. Even though it was in white primer, it still looked good!

The Coupe was originally built in Oregon but migrated to California when a G.I. was stationed at the U. S. Army base at Fort Ord, not far from Monterey. The soldier was going to be shipped out, no doubt overseas, when the Coupe was sold to LaVier's nephew. After a period of time, LaVier ended up with the Coupe.

The top had been chopped quite a bit; looked like it was done by a professional shop. Custom side panels were made, and the hood had been punched with the long style louvers. The engine was built by Tom San Paolo of Salinas. It was a 296ci Merc with an Engle cam, Edelbrock heads, and an Edelbrock manifold with three 97 carbs. The transmission had Lincoln gears; the rear end was a '48 Ford with 4.11 ratio. The front end had a dropped axle, and hydraulic brakes were used all around. Hubcaps were the popular aluminum "moon" racing discs.

The Coupe attained speeds of 96 and 99.85mph, with an elapsed time of 13.40 seconds. Racing was done at Salinas, San Jose, and the Fremont Drags. Eventually, Gordon Farnum of Monterey bought the Coupe, and then it went to someone in San Jose, California.

I heard the new owner parked the Coupe on the street in San Jose and received many parking tickets; eventually it was towed away. Within a short period of time, the Coupe was crushed and flattened to nothing! Since 1988, LaVier Van Deusen has moved from Monterey and lives in Hilmar, California.

Teaneck, New Jersey, Autorama, October 1958. Milton Lamb and son Alan presented their 1932 Chevy three-window Coupe. Painted a glade green with green-and-white upholstery, it had a Chevy six cylinder with three Stromberg carbs and a McGerk cam; it had a reported 105hp.

The top was chopped just 2 1/2in, and the only difference in the body was that the grille and shell were '32 Ford. It took the Lambs four months to build the car. Front axle and brakes were from a '40 Chevy, and the Coupe had '40 Buick bumpers and Pontiac taillights.

The Lambs were from Oceanport, New Jersey. The Coupe still exists today, but is owned by Tommy Lee of New Jersey, who also owns the Sam Barris chopped '49 Mercury.

LEFT MIDDLE

In October of 1958, I went to the Teaneck, New Jersey, car show. I showed my 1958 Chevy at the time. At that show, one of the most outstanding Roadsters was Jack Lentz's (of Belford, New Jersey) "Goldenrod" channeled '32 Ford. The channeling was 8in over the frame. The windshield was from a late stock model butted to the cowl. The front had a 2 1/2in dropped axle with '41 Ford spindles and brakes. Paint job is a twenty-coat gold tone lacquer.

Upholstery was tan-and-white Naugahyde with carpets to match. Dash was custom-made with Stewart Warner instruments; the steering wheel was '49 Ford. The engine was a '49 Mercury V–8 with dual carbs; the block was painted cream. High compression heads were Weiand finned aluminum. Note the front cycle fenders fit so closely to the tires that you can hardly see them!

OPPOSITE PAGE BOTTOM

Teaneck, New Jersey, Autorama of 1958. Benjamin F. Trimble of Mount Holly, New Jersey, is the owner of this Model "A." By the looks of the body moldings, at one time it was a Coupe. With the top cut off, it became a Roadster.

My resources tell me that Benjamin started work on the Roadster in 1952, and it was completed in 1958. The Model "A" body was either a '30 or '31 and was channeled over a '32 Ford frame. The engine was a Ford flathead, with three carbs and high compression heads. There was a 1932 Ford shell and grill in front, along with custom nerf bars. The Roadster windshield frame and stanchions were unidentifiable. Upholstery was orange-and-white Naugahyde, with upholstery lapped over the doors. The spectator was really interested in the dash!

BOTTOM

I'm sorry to say that here's another unidentified Roadster that appeared at the Rupp Chevrolet Dealership in Lynbrook, Long Island, New York, in February of 1958. This picture was sent back to New York to have a few of my friends there try to identify it. No luck!

It was a beautifully channeled '32 Ford Roadster and had a Ford or Mercury flathead with three carbs. Included were custom-made exhaust headers with metallic drag pipes underneath. An engine-turned aluminum plate was on the firewall, which gave it that custom look.

The upholstery looks like Naugahyde, in white with black pleats in the seat. Windshield looks stock height; steering wheel looks like a '48 Ford. Typical of the '50s were the wide whitewalls!

ABOVE

In February of 1958, the Rupp Chevrolet Dealership in Lynbrook, Long Island, New York, had an auto show. An outstanding '34 Ford three-window Coupe belonged to Ray Smith of Cold Springs Harbor, New York. Ray got the Coupe in 1954 and started working on it immediately. He knew what he wanted to do and started by removing the floor and channeling the body 8in over the frame. Channeled Coupes were always the fashionable thing—very racy looking. In the beginning, Ray had a '48 Mercury flathead engine in the Coupe, along with a dropped front axle and '40 Ford brakes.

When I took this picture of the Coupe, Ray had installed a 265ci Chevy engine. It had a Duntov cam, solid lifters, an Edelbrock manifold with three Stromberg 97 carbs, a Vertex magneto, and Ram's Horn exhaust manifolds. The transmission was a Corvette four speed; the rear end was a Chevy with 3.36 gears. '46 Chevy taillights graced the rear. The paint was Bahama Blue lacquer; white rolled-and-pleated upholstery was done by Foreign Custom Shop in Huntington, New York. Pinstriping was done by Ray. Custom nerf bars were designed to hold the front license plate, and note the 1958 date!

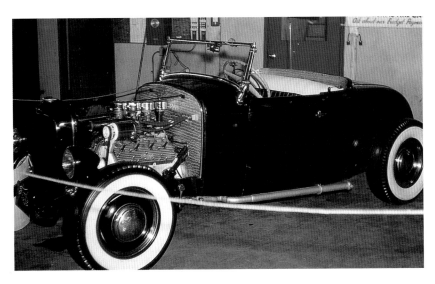

ABOVE

In February of 1959, the Rupp Chevrolet Dealership in Lynbrook, Long Island, New York, had their car show. George Tibball of Valley Stream, New York, was the owner and builder of this channeled '31 Model "A" Roadster; he is seen here wiping down his Roadster. The sign in front credits his Roadster as a 1959 Long Island Street Rod. His grille shell was a '32 Ford that had the water filler molded off; the grille was expanded metal and was painted candy red. The front axle was dropped; hydraulic brakes were all around. Looks like his windshield is chopped about 3in or more. To the right of George's Roadster is a display hood I had, showing what my pearl painting looked like with striping, scallops, and louvers. My black '58 Chevy is next to that.

The Roadster's engine was a 270ci Chevy V–8 with three carbs. The '40 Ford steering wheel was painted the same as the body. White-and-turquoise Naugahyde upholstery made a pleasing contrasting color combination. Typical of the '50s were the wide whitewalls and the baldy hubcaps. George had a fixed solid top that was white Naugahyde; the top had turquoise-and-white pleats underneath. This was a real nice East Coast Street Roadster!

February 1959, Rupp Chevrolet Dealership car show, Lynbrook, New York. The Drivin' Deuces Club of Carlstadt, New Jersey, came over with their Sierra pickup, which was highly modified and customized. Sixteen members took part in doing all the work, which took a year and a half to complete.

This '40 Ford half–ton pickup was chopped 4in and channeled over the frame 8in; the cowl and hood were sectioned. A couple of feet were taken off the end of the pickup bed. The front and rear fender wells were cut out to show off the complete tire and wheel. The tarp on the bed had the club's name and emblem stitched in for advertisement. Paint was Sierra gold lacquer.

The engine was a 296ci '48 Mercury, running an Iskenderian cam, Edelbrock heads, Weiand three-carb manifold, and custom exhaust headers and plugs. Gold velvet and Naugahyde graced the interior. Stewart Warner gauges occupied the dash and the custom panel above the windshield. Nerf bars were front and rear, with the club's name integrated in the rear nerf bars. Truly an outstanding truck for its time!

During my New York pinstriping days, I had the pleasure of striping Carl Sampogna's '32 Ford pickup. Carl owned Carl's Body Shop in Brooklyn, New York, but he lived in my home town of Oceanside. At the time, I was twenty-six–years old and had just been striping for about three years. This picture was taken in May of 1959. At the time, white pinstriping was popular, but later on he came back for more striping, at which time I added some red.

As you can see, Carl's pickup was glade green in color, sporting a '55 Buick V–8. The body was channeled over the frame. A few years later, Carl re–did the truck, adding a spare tire on the custom pickup bed; the name "La Piu Bella" was on the tire cover. Tires were changed to skinnier whitewalls; he put on bigger step plates and repainted the truck a tomato red with gold scallops.

October 21–25, 1959, Springfield, Massachusetts. The World's Fair Auto Show was produced by Joe Kizis. One of the entries was Gerald Lettieri's 1933 Ford Phaeton. He was from West Hartford, Connecticut. The information I found on the Phaeton showed that he had a full hopped–up Mercury V–8 flathead engine. The paint was a beautiful maroon, with double-line pinstriping. He also had the trendy wide whitewall tires. Upholstery was pleated, with a red-and-white motif.

Once again, the 1959 World's Fair Auto Show in Massachusetts. One outstanding Roadster was this purple '29 Ford body on a '32 Ford frame. The wheelbase was 108in, and it was non–fendered; weight was about 2,160lb. It was owned by Nelson Duchesnau of Westfield, Massachusetts.

The front end had a dropped axle, split front wishbones, a custom nerf bar with his initials, springs, and shocks. All parts were chrome-plated. Hydraulic brakes were all around. Body modifications included a filled '32 grille shell, a molded cowl on the body, molded-off door handles, rounded bottom rear trunk corners, and '39 Ford taillights. The interior had white Naugahyde rolls and pleats, and it sported accent white pinstriping on the body and grille shell.

The engine was a 251ci Mercury flathead that had a Potvin 282 cam, Evans three-carb manifold, Evans high compression heads, and a Harmon & Collins magneto ignition. Firewall was chromed. Custom outside type exhaust headers were chromed and led into an exhaust system under the Roadster.

Anybody who knows Hot Rods has heard of Dave Marasco of Carmel Valley, California. Dave built a beautiful '29 Ford Roadster pickup in the late '50s, and it was a show winner in the 1960s. But what was Dave's car before it became a Roadster pickup?

Here is a young Dave Marasco with his 1930 Ford Coupe, painted black as usual, with all the old style trimmings, wide whitewalls, and baldy hubcaps. Dave wanted a Roadster, particularly a Roadster pickup. Word was, there was one in Watsonville. He pursued it and ended up with a cab and pickup bed of '29 vintage. Supposedly, a member of the Santa Cruz Cam Snappers had the Roadster pickup at one time. So, Dave pulled off the Coupe body, and he had his Roadster pickup a year later.

Another beautiful Roadster from the West Springfield World's Fair Auto Show of 1959. John Savasta brought his channeled 1932 Ford Roadster. The body was channeled 8in over the frame. Other modifications included a proportioned 4in chopped radiator, shell, and grille. The engine is a 215ci Oldsmobile with three carbs.

John hails from Farmingham, Massachusetts, and it took three years to build his Roadster. Paint was candy apple red, and the interior was black rolled-and-pleated Naugahyde. Door hinges were flared and molded into the doors. Windshield was slightly chopped. The front wishbones look like they were split and custom-made with insert gussets for strength; they were chrome-plated. Very popular at the time was the use of Oldsmobile spinner hubcaps.

ABOVE RIGHT

On my trips to Los Angeles, I would often stop in Santa Maria to grab some lunch. This one time I spotted a clean 1946 Ford pickup truck with flames. So I had to stop, check it out, and, as usual, take some pictures.

I just recently found out that the pickup belonged to Skip Gibson of Santa Maria, who owned and operated Superior Muffler Shop on West Main Street in Santa Maria. The pickup, I understand, had a small block Chevy in it. It sported a flame job, which was popular at the time. Chrome reverse wheels with baldy hubcaps, chromed running boards, and chromed exhaust stacks going up and alongside the bed to the rear were featured.

Also popular at the time were names. "Hot Box" was put on the right rear fender. Truly a fine Rod pickup of it's era. Skip Gibson was also a member of the Santa Maria Dragons and is now deceased.

Quite often, when you read a feature about a car in an automotive magazine, you also look at the pictures presented. The majority of the time, you can see a club transfer decal on the windshield or the side vent window.

Shown here is the first decal of the Los Angeles Roadster Club. The legend is in somewhat of a script form, with the word "MEMBER" in the middle. The profile of the '32 Roadster represents Dick Scritchfield's Roadster. He was one of the founding fathers of the club.

This decal is courtesy of my good friend Greg Sharp.

The original Bay Area Roadster Decal was also in oval shape, with the San Francisco Golden Gate Bridge in the background. The front shot of the Model "A" Roadster was a takeoff on club member Paul Hannon's '29 Roadster. "MEMBER" was printed below the Model "A" grille shell. The block motif letters, "Bay Area Roadsters," were printed in gold to match the gold in the bridge. The current B.A.R. decal was modernized

some years ago by designer Don Varner. Members even have a belt buckle to match!

Decal sizes were about the same for these clubs.

In January of 1960, Gene Winfield of Modesto, California, entered his 1935 Ford Rod pickup in the San Jose Car Show.

The top was chopped 3 1/2in; the rear fenders were '39 Chevy pickup; it had ribbed aluminum on the sides of the pickup bed, and had custom taillights. It had front and rear nerf bar bumpers that were matched completely. The shortened steering column had a '56 Merc steering wheel. The custom grille was made of 5/16in steel rod, and the chromed floor of the pickup bed was birch and varnished.

Interior was gold-and-white Naugahyde. The color of the pickup was cinnamon bronze, and the inside was painted beige pearl. The engine was a flathead Mercury. A few years later, Gene took the flathead out and replaced it with a Corvette V–8 engine. Gene did all the work in his custom shop.

LEFT MIDDLE

San Jose Car Show, January 1960. Ed Roth from Maywood, California, presented his "Excaliber," a fiberglass "T" styled Roadster. Later, it became known as the "Outlaw" Roth Roadster. The engine was a '50 Cadillac that included a Cragar manifold with four 97 carbs. The engine was slightly modified. My photographs show wire wheels on the front. When it was featured in *Car Craft*, January 1960, it had solid wheels on the front. Quad headlights were from a '59 Rambler, grille was a piece from a '59 Chevy, and the windshield was from a '22 Dodge. Blue tinted safety glass was used.

Ray Silva of San Jose, California, owned this 1929 Ford Roadster pickup—an outstanding example of a Street Rod. It was driven often and was shown at most of the California car shows in the early years of car shows. It was built in the early 1950s; body work was performed by Wilhelm Custom Shop of San Jose. Ray's Roadster was probably one of the first Roadsters to have horizontal grille bars inside the 1932 grille shell.

The Ford flathead engine had Edelbrock heads and sported three carburetors. The rear end of the Silva Roadster had a Halibrand quick change center. Wide whitewalls and chromed wheels were the norm in the early Street Rod days. The red upholstery was done by Banning of Gilroy, California.

Ray was instrumental in and one of the charter members of the Bay Area Roadster Club. Ray was a good friend for many years, and we were fellow B.A.R. members. Ray passed away in 1989, and he still had his Roadster at that time—with a 283ci Chevy engine. He will be missed.

ABOVE

The Sacramento Autorama in 1960 featured Norm Grabowski's "T" Roadster pickup. Shown here with the modifications made in 1957 is the "Kookies Kar." This car was famous on the TV series "77 Sunset Strip," which starred Connie Stevens and Ed "Kookie, lend me your comb" Byrnes.

The engine was a 354ci '52 Cadillac that had a Winfield cam and four Stromberg 97 carbs. The Roadster also had a '39 Ford transmission, a '37 Ford tube front axle, a 96in wheelbase, and custom chromed headers. It featured Tony Nancy upholstery.

BELOW

Dean Jeffries performed the blue paint job and did the pinstriping. The taillights were in the bed and were from a '54 Buick. At the drag strip, it turned a speed of 103mph. Truly one of the finest classic "T"s ever built!

It was unique in styling; the top was wood framed with aluminum and Naugahyde coverings. Stewart Warner gauges enhanced the dash. A '58 Chevy steering wheel was used. Custom chrome headers complimented the pearl paint job, which was accented with turquoise and silver scallops. The frame was 90in long, and it sported a '37 Ford front axle, '41 Ford steering, '48 Ford brakes, and '58 Chevy taillight housings with '56 Chevy lenses. The rear spring from a Model "A" was on top of a '48 Ford rear end. This was the start of the trend for way–out custom Roadsters.

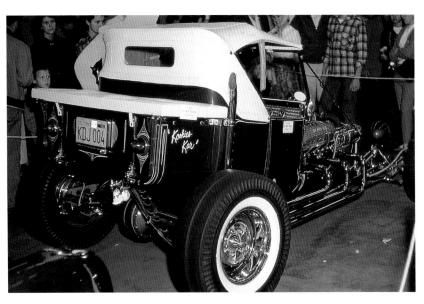

Another fantastic '32 Ford "high boy" type Coupe was this Competition five-window Ford, owned by Mason Peters of Los Gatos, California. It had a 241ci '54 Dodge V–8 engine, a '39 floor shift transmission, and a Halibrand quick change rear end. All this pushed the Coupe through the Bonneville Salt Flats at 122.78mph.

I took these pictures at the March 1960 Oakland Roadster Show. Today, the Coupe is owned by a friend of mine, John LaBelle, of Sutter Creek, California. He bought the Coupe in 1989, and it's still in the original good condition!

Rex Clark of Redding, California, owned this 1929 Ford Roadster. Painted black lacquer, it was non–fendered on a '32 Ford frame. The engine was a '55 Chevy V–8 with Jahns pistons, a Potvin cam, three carbs, and dual coil ignition. It was upholstered in gold rolled-and-pleated Naugahyde. Rex is a member of the Shasta Roadsters, Inc.

In The Background

This yellow 404 '32 Ford High Boy was built by Charlie Tabucchi Engineering in 1958. It featured a Chrysler 300 engine, 6–71 Supercharger, Winfield cam, Vertex magneto, and a '37 Buick transmission.

The Roadster was painted Golden Rod Yellow by Hal's Body Shop in San Rafael. It is the current world's record holder in A/Street Roadster Class at 136mph.

ABOVE

The Oakland Roadster Show, 1960. Sitting next to Don Brusseau's "T" was Ray Anderegg's '27 "Flip Top T." The top unsnapped in front and hinged in the rear to give easy access to the driver seat. The "T" was in a tie (with Black Gejeian's Roadster) in 1955 for the coveted title of "America's Most Beautiful Roadster." This was the first time that a tie happened.

Ray's Roadster started life as a Coupe. The top was cut off, the doors were molded into the body, and a Roadster was born. The front end was entirely chromed. The Roadster had a '56 Chevy engine with three carbs, a '39 Ford transmission, and a '41 Mercury rear end with 3.54 gears.

The interior was white Naugahyde. The body was painted a golden green lacquer with white and black design pinstriping that fit the era. Chrome wheels were reversed to clear the tires from the body. The body was channeled 4in over the frame, and the windshield was a chopped Model "A."

The interior was pearl white Naugahyde by Martinez; rugs were white. The steering wheel was '59 T–Bird. The custom dash had Stewart Warner gauges. Paint by Barris was Candy Cerise and Diamond Dust Pearl lacquer. An outstanding photo layout appeared in the July 1960 issue of *Hot Rod Magazine*.

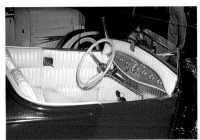

ABOVE

This picture takes us back to the Oakland Roadster Show of 1956. At that time, the Roadster was painted a light yellow and had wide whitewalls with hubcapped wheels. Dash gauges are from a '42 Buick. It was '42 Ford flathead powered and had an Evans manifold with three carbs, Offenhauser heads, and an H & C ignition. Blackie Gejeian's "T" is to the top left hand corner of the picture. The AMBR trophy sits between the Roadsters.

ABOVE RIGHT

What a sight to behold at the March 1960 Oakland Roadster Show. Here they sit in all their glory—the "Ala Kart" ('58 & '59 winner) and the new "America's Most Beautiful Roadster" of 1960, a '29 Ford owned by Chuck Krikorian of Fresno, California.

The "Ala Kart" was not in competition that year, so Richard Peters could give his brother–in–law a chance for the big trophy. They showed both cars together, side by side. What a beautiful sight it was!

It took Chuck four years to build this Roadster, with the handy work of Barris Kustom Shop. The frame originally was a '31 Ford that was taken apart and completely chromed. The body was smoothed, molded, and channeled over the frame 8in. The Roadster featured chrome reverse wheels with '50 Merc hubcaps, custom cycle fenders, a chopped custom windshield, and a nosepiece and grille shell made from 3/4in tubing and double paneled. The grille center had expanded metal with oval tubes. The oval headlights had '58 Mercury headlight buckets with plastic lenses over the concave light units. The engine was a 406ci '57 Cadillac and had a Chet Herbert cam and six 97 carbs. Everything was plated.

ABOVE

Chosen "Best Hot Rod" at the 1960 Oakland Roadster Show, Ed & Sue Ducazau's highly modified '29 Ford Roadster pickup is truly a winner.

When I saw the Roadster in 1958, it was bright red and pretty sharp. With these new changes, it looked like a different Roadster. The bottom of the body was trimmed 1in all around, and the windshield was chopped. The '32 Ford frame had the front portion removed and replaced with chrome molly tubing bent to shape to accept the front spring. The wheelbase is a long 123in. Damon Ritchey painted the Roadster maroon pearl. Alliance chrome plates, reverse wheels, and baldy hubcaps give that early style look. Custom nerf bars are bolted to the frame just in front of the rear wheels. Steering is from a '56 Ford pickup, proceeding out the driver's side of the cowl, with a drag link to the steering arm.

The engine was a 350ci 1952 Cadillac that had an Iskenderian E4 cam, Jahns pop-up pistons, a Weiand intake manifold with six carbs, and a W & H DuCoil ignition. Custom outside chrome headers were fabricated by Ed. The interior was black-and-white Naugahyde. Side panels of the bed were louvered, and the taillights were in the rear of the bed. Custom nerf bars by Ed protected the tailgate and back of the Roadster. Ed was also a member of the Long Beach Renegades Car Club.

NEXT PAGE TOP

Oakland Roadster Show, 1960. Edward Brown from Hayward, California, entered his 1950s-built custom Phaeton body '32 Ford. Originally built by Bernie J. Stein of Hayward, Bernie chopped the top off a '32 Ford Victoria to make this two-door Phaeton. King Covers of Hayward made the custom tonneau cover and reworked the interior with white Naugahyde pleats. Carpeting was done in black. The body was fitted with a custom fiberglass cowl to accommodate the custom V–type windshield. Except for the Howard cam, a stock '53 Chrysler V–8 was used.

NEXT PAGE BOTTOM

It was originally painted '57 Chrysler Cloud White lacquer. The front had custom nerf bars. Chrome reverse wheels were used. Most likely, the new owner did the pleated running boards and added the candy red paint job. Custom nerf bars on the rear were recessed, and the license plate was mounted in the middle. '39 Ford taillights were placed in the fenders. An unusual show car!

I took this picture in the early 1960s at the L.A. Roadster Club Car Show, which was at the Hollywood Bowl. The show presented a late-'50s-built touring by Norm Grabowski of Sun Valley, California.

Norm's '25 "T" touring body work was done by Valley Custom Shop in Burbank. Power was supplied by a '48 Mercury flathead, and the touring sported a Ford transmission, a 3.78 Ford rear end, and '56 Ford pickup steering. Bill Colgan's Auto Upholstery did the deep diamond tuft upholstery. Norm's touring appeared with Mamie Van Doren in the film *Sex Kittens Go To College*. Years later, the "T" was sold, and it appeared in the TV series "My Mother The Car."

In 1969, Neal East, an L.A. Roadster Club member, ended up with the Roadster. He put a flathead motor back in the Roadster. As of 1995, he still had the car. In this picture, we see Neal sitting in the Roadster at the Roadster Roundup in Visalia, California, in September 1972. You can see the flathead engine under the hood. Neal currently lives in Colorado and owns Colorado Car Books of Englewood. He has been a good friend for many years!

NEXT PAGES

One early morning in October of 1961, I was at the Hollywood Bowl in Los Angeles. The L.A. Roadster Club was presenting its Second Annual Outdoor Car Show.

One of the most outstanding Roadsters there was this black beauty that once belonged to Doane Spencer, who started this in 1938. Doane installed the DuVall V–type windshield in 1941. Doane drove the Roadster a lot, and even raced it at Dry Lakes. It's

even been said that he toured forty–two of our United States with it. I can imagine the looks it got!

After the 1950s Lakes meet, it was torn down to be set up for the Mexican Road Races. Modifications included "Z–ing" the frame front and back, installing vented Lincoln brakes, installing a quickchange rear end, running the exhaust through the side frame rails, attaching pin–drive Halibrand wheels, and installing a Lincoln

Y–block overhead valve V–8. All this was done by 1952. The steel lift-off top was done by Valley Customs in Burbank in 1950. Needless to say, it was never completed for Doane to use in the Mexican Road Races.

By 1959, the editor of *Rod & Custom Magazine*, Lynn Wineland, got the Roadster and put it back on the streets for driving. This is how it appeared when I saw it at the Hollywood Bowl.

I first met Dick Scritchfield in 1961, at the L.A. Roadster Club Outdoor Car Show at the Hollywood Bowl. I really can't remember who introduced us, but after a short time, we became very good friends and still are to this day!

His Roadster was on the cover of *Hot Rod Magazine*, back in October of 1948, when it belonged to owner/builder Bob McGee. After a front end wreck and another owner, Dick bought the Roadster in 1956. Dick added the outside headers and the FIRST red metalflake paint job. The flathead engine that McGee had was gone, and a Chevy V–8

took its place. When visiting Dick, he would give me, many times, fast and furious rides on the L.A. freeways. I especially cherish the three-minute rides from Glendale to Burbank! But maybe I'm giving away one of our secrets.

The Roadster has been seen in many films, including *Hot Rod Gang*, *Love In A Goldfish Bowl* (with the singer Fabian), and *Van Nuys Boulevard*, to mention a few, and numerous TV programs, especially "Fantasy Island," which is syndicated worldwide. It has also appeared in advertisements and magazine stories.

When I took this picture, I wanted something different. I didn't want to show the side that had the door open and the hood up, so I shot the sunny side of the Roadster. In September of 1965, I had the honor and pleasure of pinstriping the Roadster, and again later on when the Roadster was painted black.

In the 1970–71 season, it became the world's fastest Street Roadster, setting a C/SR record of 146mph at the Bonneville Salt Flats. The Roadster still exists and is owned by Bruce Meyer of Beverly Hills, California.

Original Bill NieKamp Roadster

Oakland Roadster Show Winners of the 1950s

1950	Bill NieKamp	'29 Ford Roadster
1951	Rico Squaglia	'23 Ford Roadster
1952	Bud Crackbon	'25 Ford Roadster pickup
1953	Dick Williams	'27 Ford Roadster
1954	Frank Rose	'27 Ford Roadster
1955	Blackie Gejeian	'27 Modified Ford Roadster
	Ray Anderegg	'27 Ford Roadster
1956	Eddie Bosio	'32 Ford Roadster
1957	Jerry Woodward	'29 Ford Roadster
1958	Richard Peters	'29 Ford Roadster(Ala Kart)
1959	Richard Peters	'29 Ford Roadster(Ala Kart)
1960	Chuck Krikorian	'29 Ford Roadster(Emperor)

INDEX